The
Little Blue Book
for Filmmakers

A Primer for Directors, Writers, Actors, and Producers

Carl Gottlieb and Toni Attell

Published in 2012 by Limelight Editions
An Imprint of Hal Leonard Corporation
7777 West Bluemound Road
Milwaukee, WI 53213

Trade Book Division Editorial Offices
33 Plymouth St., Montclair, NJ 07042

Printed in the United States of America
Book design by F. Lynn Bergesen

Library of Congress Cataloging-in-Publication Data
is available upon request

ISBN 978-0-87910-427-6

www.limelighteditions.com

The
Little Blue Book
for Filmmakers

Contents

Appendices

Introduction

This book is both a guide and a practical manual for the process of creating audio-visual entertainment. That includes movies, television, short videos, music videos, webisodes, mobisodes, and other Internet content. We will talk about writing, acting, directing, producing, and all the related processes, in both live action and animation. In it you will find the answers to questions of interpretation, communicating with your cocreators, managing a staff and crew, dealing with investors, and working in a hierarchy on both sides of the camera.

Years ago *The New Yorker* published a cartoon in which a pair of seals in full costume is standing by their props: three horns and a few balls. One seal is saying to the other, "Of course, what I really want to do is direct."

A director is usually a boss, a supervisor, and a leader. People who want to be directors tend to favor control and controlling. People who want to be actors or performers tend to be "people pleasers" who enjoy the spotlight, and the attention and gratification of bringing characters to life.

Writers tend to be storytellers who enjoy the control of creating a text and the pleasure of seeing that text come to life.

This is a small book with answers for large problems and shortcuts for the easy stuff. It will help you manage your subordinates, deal with your employers, and enjoy collaboration with all your partners in the creative process.

No single volume can include all there is to know, but within this book there's some hard information and specific examples that will enable you to approach the jobs of writing, directing, acting, and producing. To achieve distinction, you will need more then this book; you will need experience. A book is no substitute for experience, but it is a substitute that you can rely on until you accumulate a body of work from which to draw your inspiration.

This book began as a workbook for directors, and an introductory primer for film students and others interested in filmmaking. As it evolved, we realized the importance of including information and insight into all the related arts of making movies. Along the way, we found ourselves using a lot of military metaphors. We're not militarists or reflexive authoritarians, but we found ourselves returning, again and again, to the peculiar requirements and insular hierarchical nature of show business. It's not for nothing that old-timers in show business refer to everyone outside the profession as "civilians." Like the military or the church, show business is a calling; hardly anyone enters the profession by accident; we all volunteered. Many are called, but few are chosen.

If you want to be a director, you'll be at the center of everything, but remember: a bull's-eye in the middle of a target is also at the center of everything, and it's what everyone aims at when they shoot. And if that analogy isn't enough, consider that being at the top means everything else is holding you up, and if that support fails, you fall long and hit hard. Once at the top, the only defense against falling is to go further. As actor Larry Hankin once said, "'Full out' is the only protection for 'go ahead.'"

If you're comfortable being on top and at the center, you are probably temperamentally suited to the job of directing. What you need to know, more than anything else, is that you don't do the job alone.

You work with a script that's the work of a writer; with actors who breathe life into the characters and are practicing their own special craft; and there's a production team that put the project together, found the money to put you behind the camera, and will assemble the various craftspeople who will help you light, shoot, edit, and score the production. Nobody makes a film alone, unless he or she is a solo cartoonist or animator who works in solitary isolation with only the camera as a partner.

A great director said: "There are two categories of artists: the artists of absolute creation and those who create upon the creation of others. Our job is to understand what these great absolute artists have created, and communicate that to a public. The greatest director of 'Don Giovanni' will never be the equal of Mozart. There is a diabolical danger in the craft of interpretation, to believe that we are as capable, or even better than Mozart or Shakespeare."*

---

* Giorgio Strehler, famed Italian founder of the Piccolo Theatro di Milano, General Manager of the La Scala Opera House, and director of the Theatre de L'Europe in Paris, quoted in his obituary in the *New York Times*.

Simply put, writers and composers are artists of creation; directors and actors are artists of interpretation. Among the artists of interpretation, the director is the first among equals; as director Sam Fuller said: "The director's job is to finish the story that excited him; remember the heart of the story." In other words, one must hold to a unifying vision.

At the same time, even while acknowledging that the director is an artist of interpretation, a film director may direct, edit, even score his or her own script, or illuminate and enhance a text to such a remarkable degree that he or she may be called an *auteur* by the French, who use the term to define a film artist with a distinct and identifiable personal style. The usual suspects (and subjects) of the auteur theory are well known: Hitchcock, Ford, Peckinpah, Truffaut, Fellini, Antonioni, Altman, Kurosawa, and Bergman leap to mind.

Less well known are the geniuses (many from the era of the studio system) who could direct in any style a script demanded: Curtiz, Fleming, Schlesinger, MacKendrick, Zinneman, Lumet, and Kazan. And of course, there are those who've made such original films that they transcend auteur-journeyman pigeonholes: Ang Lee, Woody Allen, Mike Leigh, Stanley Kubrick, Francis Coppola, and the preternaturally talented Steven Spielberg. These lists are minimal; there are at least a hundred other masters from whom you can draw inspiration.

Begin with baby steps (how else do we start moving through life?), and pick some film that speaks to you and simply imitate for a bit—just as student artists copy old masters or a young comedian memorizes a successful comic's routine. A filmmaker's inspiration can come from anything the masters have done: a visual style (think John Ford's and David Lean's landscapes), verbal delivery (Woody Allen's kvetchers, Diablo Cody's teenagers), developing a story by improvising with actors (Mike Leigh), fantastical exaggeration (Fellini's *Roma*, Tim Burton's dark fairytales, the Wachowski brothers' *Matrix*, Tarantino's gangsters, and Scorsese's Mafia families).

There are a number of references here to vintage films made decades ago; they're all cataloged and summarized online (IMDB.com) and in standard reference texts (Leonard Maltin's books are the most widely circulated and available, but like most film writers, he tends to identify films by their directors and omits writers as creators, although they're all properly credited in the body of the text. More importantly, the films referenced in these pages are generally available for viewing, and if there are any you haven't seen, we urge you to look at them any way you can without resorting to bootlegs or "free" downloads that fail to compensate rights-holders. Some of the epics benefit from being seen in the format for which they were created—specifically, theatrical feature films that were made for the big screen and projected in a theater. For the whole list, see appendix E.

In this book, we'll be discussing all the challenges you will face as a filmmaker. These include time and budget constraints, capturing the visuals that enhance and expand the story, and finally, dealing with the human beings whose collaboration and contributions are essential to the ultimate work: the cast and crew. The solutions to the many problems you face will all become part of the finished product. The audience may never personally experience your problems, and while few people want to hear details of the pain of childbirth, everyone admires the newborn baby, which is your work. Memory is an imperfect journal of experience, but as we recall it, here's what you will need to know.

The
Little Blue Book
for Filmmakers

CHAPTER 1

Getting Started: Being "The Boss"

For the purposes of this chapter, let's assume that you have taken on the responsibility of being a director. Either you were hired to do the job, or you decided to make your own project, or a group (cooperative or collective) has decided that you should have the title and the responsibility. Now what?

Here's a checklist of things you will need:

- ✓ a script
- ✓ a producer
- ✓ legal counsel
- ✓ a camera
- ✓ a cast
- ✓ an editor
- ✓ a crew
- ✓ time
- ✓ money

Once your lawyer has approved the contracts, you can point the camera with the help of the crew and record the actors who are performing the script. Then you can edit the results until the producer confirms that you have run out of time and money, at which point you may consider your project finished. Now what? You'll need some more things. Here's another checklist:

✓ more legal counsel
✓ a means of distribution
✓ a sales agent for the project
✓ a marketing plan
✓ a publicist
✓ an accountant

Your producer will find a distributor with the means of distribution, while a sales agent aided by a marketing plan and the publicist will find an income stream that your accountant and lawyer will approve.

You can also surround yourself with either of two kinds of colleagues: those who share your vision and work to reinforce it, or those who have their own individual viewpoints which you can consider, choose, or reject. In both cases, film's a collaborative medium; don't ever forget that.

Many of these items overlap. The simplicity of checklists is trumped by reality, every time. With a webcam and a laptop you can write your own script, produce it, play the leading role (or every role, if you want), and perform most of the other functions all by yourself. The only exception is legal counsel, and an old cliché applies here: "A person who represents himself has a fool for a client." Never make your own deals if you can avoid it. You can do everything else by yourself, but it's more fun (and more complicated) to work and play well with others. If you don't have a professional agent, a nimble-minded friend with a skeptical nature will do. In any event, negotiating by yourself for yourself is challenging at best and ruinous at worst. How *does* one proceed? A little history first.

Most textbooks on film theory and practice assume that the reader enjoys a familiarity with the process. Historically movies began simply, as anarchic exhibitors (owners of nickelodeons and movie houses) combined forces and functions to guarantee a steady flow of product to their new ventures. They became corporate entities, formed vast theater chains, built large studios, and maintained a sales presence in every major market, both in North America and globally. They institutionalized their practices into what became "The Studio System" or "Hollywood," a growth model that was duplicated worldwide, each country developing its own version. Their descendants still haunt the horizon, huge corporate shells named Paramount, Fox, Universal, Warner Brothers, RKO, Columbia, and MGM; and Gaumont, Lumiere, Rank, Odeon, Pathe, Toho, UFA, and the like. Some were independent of theater owners (Universal, United Artists, and Columbia), but all enjoyed a near-monopoly of the means of production and distribution. Much of the vocabulary, custom, and practice still in use today can find its roots in those early decades before and after the Great War (1914–1918).

Then came the first Next Big Thing, a technological innovation called radio. This eventually gave birth to television, a mass-market medium and a sponsor-supported free alternative to the movies. There was early synergy as stars crossed over and evolved; movie stars appeared on network radio, radio stars graduated to television, and some television and radio stars became film stars. All of the broadcast media drew on an enormous talent pool of live entertainers who worked in vaudeville, a parallel performance art that flourished before movies and coexisted with them for a while. Vaudeville eventually died, as theater owners preferred the mechanical perfection of film to the messy business of booking and nurturing individual acts and performers who could not physically compete for five shows a day, seven days a week, with constant traveling between engagements. Like the movies, vaudeville and live theater had consolidated and developed an industrial model (the Keith-Albee and Orpheum Circuits, the Shubert and Pantages Theatres), and most of the early movie "palaces" played vaudeville bills as well. By the 1930s vaudeville was out, and movies ruled the nation's cities. Vaudeville stars with good voices and a strong following made the transition to broadcasting successfully, giving us Bob Hope, Jack Benny, Ed Wynn, Red Skelton, George Burns and Gracie Allen, and hundreds more, while some acts, such as the Marx Brothers, W. C. Fields, Mae West, and others, went straight into films with equal success.

Vaudeville, the movies, radio, and television were all institutionalized, followed corporate models, and made large amounts of money, joining their traditional corporate cousins on the

Dow Jones Index (manufacturing, oil and gas, transportation, pharmaceuticals, utilities, etc.) Their work forces were unionized in reaction to exploitation and abuse, their shares traded on the stock exchanges of the world.

Eventually, as in galaxies and solar systems, the constant expansion of the business of mass entertainment led to dysfunction, explosion, fragmentation, reconsolidation, and recombination, and again opened the gates to individuals with the talent, drive, or unique product required for admission. As this is written, in the second decade of the twenty-first century, that process of fragmentation and reconsolidation is proceeding at a ferocious pace. We have returned to an early evolutionary state, where hundreds of variants reproduce and mutate in a blindly choreographed effort to create new species, new forms, and successful versions of broken existing standards.

The old monolithic studios are in economic disarray; new distribution platforms are creating or delivering content for free, or at unsustainable bargain rates; and the hierarchical structures of agents, managers, talent, bookers, buyers, and producers are collapsing on themselves. Synergy is matched by dysfunction; bubbles and crashes are everywhere.

Given this state of chaos in which the individual voice struggles to be recognized, how do you—the new filmmaker— begin your career? Specifically, exactly... what do you do to get going? Forgive us for including what may seem obvious, but nobody's background and education is the same, so we're setting forth some of the history and practices that, in our opinion, will be most useful to you as you begin your journey.

Here's how you start:

- Find another business or trade or skill that will enable you to survive after your initial failures and to support yourself in the interim during which you learn your craft and others recognize your value. It's also a way to accumulate the resources you'll need to self-finance your work.

- Ignore the implications of the preceding paragraph and have unshakable confidence in your ability to persevere and triumph over all odds.

- Learn the often-mocked social skills of networking, politicking, and shameless self-promotion. You can't control what others say about you, but you can always say good things about yourself, with or without being asked. It helps if you know when to shut up.

- At the same time as you're working on 1 through 3 above, *find a project*. This can be as simple as creating something yourself—write a story, tell a joke, or find a fascinating object, animal, person, or activity on which you can focus your attention.

- Trust yourself to find inspiration and creativity anywhere: dreams, a construction project, a talkative stranger, a peculiar circumstance, an odd environment, unusual behavior, or even...real life (a personal experience, a news account, a historical event).

- Develop the project: give it form, shape, and substance. Flesh it out, give it a mood or feeling or theme. At the very least, you should be able to describe it very simply to the next person who asks you, "What're you doing these days?" ("I read this book about a shark that terrorizes a resort town and three guys go to sea in a fishing boat to catch it or kill it . . .") (See *Jaws*.)

- Get others involved. This can range from picking up a crew of fellow students or unemployed friends, to pitching your idea successfully to a source of major financing and distribution, and everything in between. You may self-finance a small production in the hope of attracting funds to recreate it in a grander version; stage workshop readings; or circulate the script to anyone who'll read it. However you go about it, have unshakable faith in the viability and necessity of production. Or at least pretend it's true.

- Learn when to suspend work on one project and start another; there will come a point when no one wants to hear your pitch again, *ever*. Put it aside, go on to something else. You're a creative person, and unless you're monomaniacal or obsessive, you will not have just one idea in your life. Good ideas and projects never die; they may sleep until the time is right or a new era begins, or until everyone forgets, but they will always be viable in one form or another. This seems not to be the case for series network television Westerns, but for everything else—keep hoping.

- Expect, believe, and have faith that one day you will step onto a stage or location with a camera, cast, and crew—even if it's your webcam, yourself, and a room; or a green-screen and a digital camera; or some available animation technology (stop-motion or drawing cells by hand).

When that day comes, you'll have this book in your pocket or your memory, and you'll proceed with confidence. Trust us. Or just fake it.

CHAPTER 2

Say Hello:
On-Set Relationships

Give yourself a moment to introduce yourself. Shaking someone's hand is the beginning of creating a relationship. In any complex creative involvement, the director is "the boss," and has to remain in control but must always remember the actor's contribution. In a Freudian sense, the director is a surrogate parent, and in this role the actor will do anything to please the boss/mother/father. In defense of non-Freudian actors, they will certainly do their best if they feel they're working together toward a common goal: a good (or commercially successful; the two aren't exclusive) movie, television show, or commercial—whatever the project. In most modern filmmaking, the director is usually seen as a dominating presence and the actor as an instrument in the realization of the work. In low-budget and student productions, the hierarchy is far less structured and there's a lot of role switching. Nevertheless, on any particular set, the rules and the roles ought to be defined and respected by all the players.

The particular relationship of director and actor is its own creative unit. The boss is usually busy with many matters, carrying on a running dialog with the director of photography (cinematographer or cameraman), the various department heads (props, grips, wranglers, transportation, etc.), perhaps even a second unit. There may also be "The Suits" (production, studio, financing, publicity, marketing, and distribution executives), who require their own special kind of attention. It helps keep a set running smoothly if you choose an actor who is prepared and able to take direction easily; pick one of these and you're ahead of the game. It is always a good idea to set up that relationship at the onset of the shoot, so if there are questions, you can answer them with the actor before moving on to the million other things that will need your attention. Be aware of the actor who can be a psychic vampire, constantly needing and diverting your focus, direction, and energy. If there's one primary lesson for dealing with actors and others, it's this: set your boundaries immediately and clearly.

This definition of roles and boundaries begins at the inception of the project. Whatever the final product, there's a moment in time when it goes from being an intangible abstract (a script, an idea, a storyboard, an assignment) to a tangible and definable property, project, or "work." It has a title; a budget; an agreed-upon story or through line; a start date; a projected completion date; a postproduction, marketing, and release schedule. Whatever the scale of the production, whether student short film or major studio theatrical feature, the essential elements remain the same. In the world of television production, there are nuances and differences to the process. These are a function of episodic or continuing storylines using the same principal actors, and with a consistency of writing and producing dictated by the broadcast schedule. Television is an ongoing process with many stories, while individual films and commercials are generally "one-offs," complete unto themselves (until the sequels).

There are a variety of personal styles for establishing the boss's overall authority. In a professional production, the hierarchy is historically well established: the director of a feature-length film is god-king (even if only unto himself). Every department reports to the director, who is the ultimate authority on what is approved or rejected. You will find that this is a blessing if you are concerned with maintaining a central directorial vision and being an auteur, and a curse, as you are asked about the color of the drapes, an actor's manicure, or what kind of pistol to give the villain.

Most professional productions are divided into two categories separated by a categorical boundary: "the line." Everyone works either *above the line* or *below the line*. What is the line? It's that division of the production budget that separates "creative" or "executive" talent from all the crafts, trades, and physical tools of production. The producer, director, actors, writer(s), literary rights, and music are "above the line," whereas the cinematographer, production designer, composer, editor, sets, locations, travel, casting, and every other element are "below the line."

The below-the-line elements have been disciplined by time and custom to honor the position of director with semimilitary discipline; their respect is for the uniform (rank) and not the person, although (as in the military) the troops will follow a leader who inspires love and respect into hell, without questioning or second thoughts. A director, like a military leader, comes cloaked with an inherent authority defined by the position. Abuse that authority—or be seen as vacillating, weak, or incompetent—and the troops will mutiny, usually to the detriment of the project.

The military commander's authority is protected by a tradition of discipline that permits the death penalty for mutiny; directors aren't so lucky. If they have lost the respect of cast and crew to the point of disobedience or apathy, they must rely on simple professionalism to maintain momentum and complete the project. The director must then appeal to all the members of the unit to put aside their personal animosities and remember the obligations of the profession: to finish the job. Long after the rebellious crew has wrapped the set and the unhappy actors have gone home to look for other work, the director remains behind to finish postproduction. In the independent or low-budget arena, where the director is also a producer/writer, the ability to maintain continuity and persist to completion is not only a virtue but a necessity.

Ideally, the situation should never be allowed to deteriorate to the point of near-mutiny or sullen apathy. Here are simple rules to avoid that disaster:

- *From the very beginning, acknowledge and respect every collaborator in the process.* At first this may be limited to writers and producers and financiers, but ultimately it includes every worker on the project, from the humblest extra to the most independent teamster.

- *Don't be fawning or obsequious.* Nobody likes an obvious ass-kisser. (Which is not to say you can't be nice and say "please" and "thank you." All the rules of common courtesy apply, even to the boss).

- *You can't know everything.* Leave the details to the professionals whose job or department is involved. For example: tell everyone that the camera will be looking in a certain direction, and then let the cinematographer set the lights and the AD and transportation captain park the trucks; chances are they've been doing those jobs for a while. Similarly, wardrobe, makeup, and hair are most responsive to generalities ("She looks a little shiny," "The zipper is showing," and "I can see his toupee.") Trust them to work their magic while you concentrate on your work as director. Above all, don't insist on doing anything a stunt coordinator or transportation captain tells you is unsafe. Sometimes "Faster!" is not an option.

- *Be prepared.* Some directors come to the set with a shot list that defines the day's work already written, others will concentrate on a master or the first setup and improvise the rest; some will shoot rehearsals, others will rehearse intensely and hope for the best when the camera's rolling. There are many methods of achieving the same goals, but they all require focus and attention to detail.

- *Don't overshare.* Your personal anxieties, doubts, experiences, and musings are not for general consumption. To return to the military metaphor, there is something called "the loneliness of command," which is an eloquent description of the necessary distance between captain and crew; officer and enlisted man; and yes, the director and cast and crew.

- *Consider the welfare of the company.* To do their best, a cast and crew must be fed and rested and relaxed. Even when conditions are difficult (distant locations, environmental extremes, long hours, short budgets), remain constantly aware of the basic needs of most people: food, shelter, clothing, and a freedom from anxiety, which means a minimum of stressful shouting and a maximum of consistent attitude. Your cast and crew want to please you; if they don't know what makes you happy or you're constantly changing priorities, they will become nervous, then afraid, then angry, and finally catatonic, which (of course) is not good. A simple matter, often overlooked, is to make sure the company follows the rules of basic hygiene, which means caterers who wash their hands, and inoculations and standby medical personnel where necessary.

- *Know your own limits.* If you need sleep, make sure you get it. If you're hungry, eat. If you don't know what's happening, find out. If you're one of those people who are validated by sexual contact, find it off the set. Sexual favors are a debased currency that buy nothing, and create unnecessary

problems. Comfort yourself with what Lord Chesterfield
said about sex: "The pleasure is momentary, the position
ridiculous, and the expense damnable."

- *Understand that the unique demands of directing sometimes
play havoc with personal and professional relationships.*
Spouses, children, and old friends need to understand you've
made a choice, and your immediate (and only) priority is
successfully completing the project; everything else is
secondary. If they love you, they'll understand. You can
make it up to them later.

- *Listen! Observe!* Try to see and hear everything around you
(a formidable chore). You will be a much more effective
boss if you actually hear the concerns of your cast and
crew, if you can see the physical obstacles confronting the
production, and if you understand the concerns of producers,
financiers, and marketing executives. This is not to say
you must personally address every issue, but at the least
you must be able to differentiate between problems and
assign priorities for solutions. If you must have a battle,
pick the site and choose your weapons carefully. Trust your
allies, and know your enemies. On the most basic level, if a
stunt or effect has the slightest element of danger, inform
the actor and be sure the crew is aware and responsible.
This is as true for low-budget or no-budget productions of
fictional or scripted material as it is true for "reality" shows
in which contestants run through obstacle courses or dance
beyond their skills or limits.

- *When all is said and done, be prepared to put your job on the line.* If anyone insists or overrides on issues of health and safety, simply stop shooting until common sense returns, or a legal or union intervention resolves the conflict. There is no artistic or aesthetic goal that justifies death or injury on the set, and you will make no friends if your first question after an accident is "Did you get the shot?"

CHAPTER 3

Picking Your Team,
Including Casting

We've been hammering the idea that filmmaking is a collaborative effort. Luckily for you, bosses have considerable discretion in the selection of their collaborative partners. With the exception of the first writer (the "artist of original creation") and the producer who owns or controls "the property," everyone who joins the production team later is usually recruited or employed with the consent of the director, or at least with his or her consultation. The DGA contract permits an exception and dictates specific work experience for the first assistant director (First AD or AD), who is technically the employee of the production department or producer and reports to them. The reason for this is simple: the AD (in collaboration with the line producer or production manager) makes many decisions that directly impact the budget and schedule, and is therefore responsible for the production's overall financial and physical well-being.

On a large-budget motion picture, the credits can take as long as twelve to fifteen minutes to unroll at the end of the film and may include, literally, a thousand names. There are dozens of categories that are listed as parts of preproduction, production, and postproduction. Specialized talents abound; there may be choreographers, dialog coaches, teachers, caterers, nurses, fencing masters and armorers, fight coordinators, stunt drivers and stunt coordinators, animal trainers, airplane and helicopter pilots, sailing instructors, dive masters, travel agents, specialized liaisons, and a hundred more. We can't enumerate them all. But every production requires a number of specific talents. In low-budget productions, one person may wear a dozen hats, and it's possible (and customary) to make a small feature film with very few people.

It's important to trust your crew members to know and do their jobs. For example, a novice director was scouting locations in the remote Southwestern desert with a seasoned crew of professionals. Like many new directors, he wanted to find locations that would be unique and special to him. So he dragged the crew by van, four-wheel drive jeeps, and finally on horseback, until he came to a slightly wooded hillside overlooking a magnificent vista. Viewfinder to his eye, he made a great deal of fuss about finding just the right place from which to make the shot. "Right here," he said to the cinematographer, Lucien Ballard. Ballard eyed the shot, moved around the clearing, and kicked away some loose brush, revealing a rusted camera tie-down still screwed into the ground. "You might consider this," he said to the director. "When I was here with Peckinpah, we put the camera right here." Ballard had never said a word the whole trip, even though he remembered the area perfectly. Sometimes you can save a half day of riding in the wilderness just by asking, "Where would be a good place to shoot the scene?"

Working from the top down or the inside out, your key personnel will be as follows:

- **Producer(s):** This is usually out of your control, and it includes people who find the money, people who find the talent, and people who control the literary property, the author, and perhaps the star. Technically, the ultimate hiring and firing authority.

- **Line Producer:** What used to be called a production manager, this is an indispensable member of the team, bearing ultimate responsibility for every physical aspect of production: budget, schedule, locations, payroll, staffing, catering, travel, and the like.

- **Associate Producer(s):** It pays to keep in mind the old Hollywood saying: "An associate producer is anyone who will associate with a producer." This is an amorphous category that runs the gamut from simple gofers to sophisticated production personnel and financial managers. It is a catchall expression to cover people whose contribution is significant to the production team in general and the producers specifically.

- **Director of Photography (DP):** Also known as cameraman or cinematographer, this is the individual completely responsible for the recorded image, whether on film, digital media, or video. This is the only job in the motion picture industry that can't be faked. DPs tend to have extensive experience and complete familiarity with every tool of their trade; from the camera to the lights and special effects, everything that is seen in the frame is ultimately the responsibility of the DP. The DP is the director's closest collaborator and is sometimes the director him- or herself. He or she must literally be the eyes of the director. The DP's team includes camera operator(s), gaffer, key grip, and dolly grip—and anyone else whose hands affect the visual image, which brings us to:

- **Production Designer:** This is a job that doesn't much exist in low-budget productions. There is usually not enough money to pay a qualified artist to be responsible for the physical look of the entire film. In studio and high-budget productions, the production designer reports to the director and producer and works very closely with the DP. They share the responsibility for every visual development on screen. In student films, shorts, and low-budget productions, the DP is the de facto production designer.

- **Costume Designer:** Like the production designer, this job is a luxury not found in low-budget productions. A costume designer, working in tandem with the production designer, is responsible for every item of wardrobe in the film. The production and costume designer work together to supervise the art department, makeup, hair, and occasionally hand props (fans, handkerchiefs, canes, etc.). It should be pointed out that production design and costume design are not limited to period or fantasy films. A contemporary film can be highly designed without appearing to be.

- **Art Director:** The art director is responsible for design and construction of all the scenic elements of the production if he or she reports to the production designer (if there is one). Otherwise the art director comes after the cameraman and follows the director and cameraman's instruction as to the look of the film.

- **Assistant Director (AD):** This job title is a misnomer; the AD doesn't really "help the director." He or she is the producer's physical representative on the set and the overlord of the crew. Every department is bossed by the AD, who translates the director's wishes into specific orders to every department (grips, electric, props, drivers, makeup and hair, wardrobe, extras, etc.). The AD usually has an assistant called a second AD, whose responsibility in the command structure is more limited. The second AD is responsible for bringing actors to the set with call times, the call sheet itself, and extras and background artists. On large productions there are additional personnel referred to as second second ADs. Production assistant(s) on the set report to the AD.

- **Script Supervisor:** This is the least understood and one of the most demanding of production jobs. The script supervisor observes everything that is being recorded or photographed and makes sure that it conforms with the script. It is also the script supervisor's job or responsibility to maintain continuity—that is, to make sure that every action and detail is consistent with everything that has been shot before, which includes even such tiny details as the length of ash on a cigarette, the level of liquid in a glass, and which hand the actor uses for a gesture. The script supervisor must record every shot in a scene, the lens used, and the director's selection of favored shots. In the old studio days, the script supervisor also prepared the daily production report, which is a record of how the day's work was accomplished (call time, time of the first shot, time used on setups, etc.).

- **Editor:** The person or persons responsible for assembling every sequence of the film into a coherent whole. The editor works closely with the director, who selects the takes to be used, and with the cinematographer to make sure there is complete coverage of each scene. The editor is usually on the payroll from the first day of shooting through the delivery of the final cut. A highly technical specialty with its own demanding rules, editing can be crucial to the success of a project. An editor (at least in the initial cut or assembly) is responsible for the pace and timing of the picture. Although great editors have been credited with "saving" a picture, it should be remembered that every image that an editor works with was originally chosen by a director and shot by a cinematographer. In other words, an editor can only work with the elements with which he or she has been provided. Some directors (Woody Allen comes to mind) make it a point to budget for "reshoots" and additional photography during the postproduction editing process, so as to be able to create elements that were overlooked during shooting or that become apparently necessary in assembling the finished product. Editors work alone or with a few assistants, far from the bustle of the set; they tend to be happy loners.

- **Composer:** If a picture is to have any original music as underscoring or accompaniment, the composition of that score is the responsibility of the composer. The composer works with the director and editorial department in the final stages of postproduction and is one of the few "artists of original creation" in the collaborative process. He or she must not only have a complete grasp of musical composition but also understand the technical requirements of writing short *cues*, which are fragmentary bits of music that accompany the action on the screen. The number of composers who can competently score a film is limited. Because of the constraints of time and budget, a composer's work is the last creative addition to the film, and there is rarely time or money to redo a score. Hence, composers for film must be able to get it right the first time, every time. Because musical scoring has a huge effect on the audience's experience of the film, it is a vital component and cannot be left to chance or delegated to novices. In low-budget films, a **music coordinator** can substitute for the composer.

- **Music Coordinator:** He or she is responsible for finding and licensing existing music to lay on the soundtrack without the luxury of original composition. In large-budget films, the music coordinator works with the composer to provide a seamless musical score for the soundtrack, consisting of both original and prerecorded cues. The director usually consults with the composer as to mood and timing of the music, and may even provide a *temp track* consisting of recorded music that is similar to what the director envisions in the final version.

The other key elements of the production team are defined by their departments:

- **Location Manager:** Finds the locations, secures the property owner's permission, and obtains permits and insurance policies that are required by local jurisdictions.

- **Casting Director:** Finds and prescreens talent for every part in the film, works with the director and producers in suggesting actors for the principal roles, and negotiates fees with agents and managers for all but the highest-paid stars. The casting director also maintains ongoing relationships with agents and managers between productions, and actively scouts sources of new talents—i.e., little theater productions, talent shows, workshop productions, and so forth.

- **Makeup, Hair, and Wardrobe Departments:** Are self-defined as an individual or team that is responsible for each of those specialized elements of the production.

- The same goes for **Transportation, Electric, Grip,** and **Props**.

- **Craft Services:** Responsible for set maintenance and onstage availability of snacks.

- **Caterer:** Responsible for preparing, serving, and cleaning up scheduled meals for cast, crew, and extras.

- **Wranglers:** Responsible for livestock and any other animals used in production (including reptiles and insects).

- **Postproduction Supervisor:** Works with the editor and all the elements that are added after the principal photography is completed. These include: additional visual effects, sound editing, postproduction dialog (ADR and looping), sound effects, voiceover narration, graphics, titles, and special effects.

- **Production Assistant (PA):** This is the lowest rung on the ladder of production and is usually an entry-level job, sometimes filled by unpaid interns. PAs are paid less and work longer hours than most of the production team, which explains why the PA is one of the few nonunion jobs open on a commercial production. In student and short films, PAs aren't worked as hard because they tend to be totally unpaid volunteers and recognized only in the credits. Sub-categories of PAs are found, on set, in the production office, on locations, and in pre- and postproduction.

The oft-quoted serenity prayer is something that all leaders (including directors) should take to heart: "God grant me the serenity to accept the things I cannot change, the courage to change the things I can, and the wisdom to know the difference."

In picking a team, the most appropriate analogy is that you are a commander leading troops into the field on a special mission. Your mission is to make your film. Unlike in combat, there is no one actively seeking to kill you and destroy your unit. Like in combat, unforeseen circumstances and the true capabilities and limitations of your team are never completely known. Wind and weather can conspire against you, people you thought were heroes may turn out to be villains or cowards, and great accomplishments may be achieved by heroes that you didn't know you had.

The selection of your crew (team, posse, gang, company) is a process that involves as much luck as it does skill. In a perfect world, you would know every member of the crew, have worked with them before, and have trust and knowledge of their abilities and limitations. They would all be amiable, hardworking, cooperative, and supportive. If you are lucky or blessed, you will have several occasions in a lifetime to work with such a crew. However, it is not a perfect world. In most other ventures, the director will have the power to hire and fire most members of the crew and cast. This authority may be shared with the producers or financiers and the occasional key department head—such as the cinematographer, who usually insists on bringing his or her own crew.

Consequently, any crew is a somewhat random collection of individuals who are assembled for the single purpose of completing the project that began with a script.

Keep in mind that in certain environments, particularly episodic television, the director is simply a senior member of a team—a boss, not *the* boss. If you are offered such a job, you should accept the fact that you may be a subordinate player. There are people over you whose authority exceeds your own; if you can't accept that fact, you should not take the job.

With the exception noted above, you as the director must assume personal responsibility for all the personal choices over which you have authority. Without direct experience, how can you tell if someone is a hard worker—self-motivated, energetic, and clever—or a slacker who will do the minimum required of him or her to collect a paycheck. Of course you check backgrounds and references. A director should never engage a cinematographer without physically viewing his or her work and discussing the problems and charms of the project at hand. For example, if your project is a snowy ski adventure, you would be wary of hiring a cinematographer whose entire reel consists of beautifully lit, controlled interiors. Occasionally a team member's enthusiasm and love for a project will overcome a lack of experience.

Keep in mind that in show business, everyone is a skilled seducer. Personal charm is one of the entry-level requirements, and enthusiasm can be faked. Even experience is suspect in a collaborative medium where many contributors have participated in a single project. More than once, the authors have viewed competing reels submitted by cinematographers and visual-effects specialists that include the same shot. This may not be deception: they may each have worked on an aspect of the film they are submitting and be entitled to take credit for it;

sometimes their experience in making the shot on their reel is an exaggeration or simply a misstatement of the facts. The lesson here is to personally check all references.

In underfunded or independent productions and short films, members of the crew will frequently have multiple responsibilities and not much depth of experience. In these cases, enthusiasm may be the only valid substitute for experience. In every case where you make choices for your team, including casting of actors, it is important to pay attention to your instinctive, intuitive, and spontaneous reactions to anyone you're meeting. As Gavin DeBecker says in his book *The Gift of Fear*, "Evolution has supplied us with an innate and instinctive reaction to threat or danger." In his book, which is about stalkers, his context is one of self-defense and protection. In the context of team selection and picking a crew, the positive side of this equation is more important. Naturally, you are not going to hire anyone you instinctively fear. On the other hand, if a person has an innate charm and appeal to you, that is a powerful positive factor on his or her behalf. All things being equal, hire people you think you like or who appear to be folks you'd like to spend time with. Everyone on your crew should be a suitable companion on a lifeboat or desert island where they have the skills you need to survive and succeed—and a personality that doesn't make you want to kill them.

As a director, you'll get the feeling from time to time that many of your crew *would* like to kill you. That comes with the territory. It is part of the loneliness and responsibility of command, and since you're neither on a polar expedition nor in mortal combat, it doesn't matter. After all, as Alfred Hitchcock said to Ernest Lehman during the making of *North by Northwest*, "Ernie, relax—it's just a movie."

However, since no one in a collaborative process can be truly alone or work without support, the boss should maintain cordial, even dependent relationships with a senior member or members of the crew. The people best qualified to cover your back are usually the AD, unit manager or line producer, cinematographer, sometimes the script supervisor—anyone who is in a central position of some authority with an overview of the entire production. Sometimes a trusted friend or confidante may be enlisted into the crew for this purpose. The person or persons who cover your back have to be trusted to do their job without appearing to be rats or snitches, or to be taking advantage of their position. They have to do their job properly if they are to be trusted to protect you. In this situation, use your common sense; the people who are helping are doing you no favors if they are antagonizing the crew or abusing their privileged access to you.

This brings us to the subject of nepotism, for which show business is famous. Curiously, no one objects when lawyers, farmers, shoemakers and bakers teach their children their trade or craft. In fact the legend "& Son"—or in the case of the New York delicatessen, "Russ and Daughters"—reflects a proud addition to the name of the firm. Why then should anyone object to multiple generations of Zanucks, Barrymores, Carradines, Bridges, Zemeckes, Coppolas, and the like? After all, if you trust your spouses, siblings, and children enough to bring them into show business, you should trust them enough to watch your back in a production in which you are involved (or your winery). The family ties are important, and blood relationships are something that can transcend most differences and antagonisms. Furthermore, if you're bringing a family member onto the team, what better teacher or instructor could they ask for (assuming you know your job). This is true whether they are actors or working on your production team.

Actors are not a breed apart. They are invaluable contributing members of the crew, and everything said here applies to them as well. In addition, actors are picked for their unique ability to portray a character, which is 95 percent of their job, which is why bad behavior, temperament, and ignorance may be excused if they're right for the part. You can replace a director, but you can't replace the only actor in the world who can play the part. Luckily there are very few parts that can be played by only one actor. They, too, are replaceable. Except after production has begun and they are established on film. The only time a principal actor is replaceable after filming starts is when he or she dies. Which brings us to the single most important selection process in which the director is intimately involved: casting.

Previously, we mentioned the casting director as an integral part of the team. Along with the production designer and location scouts, the casting director is one of the first staff members to be engaged. In the studio days, the casting office was open year round and serviced all the productions on the lot. In this era of scaled-back production, casting director(s) (they often work in pairs) are fee-based independent contractors who perform a variety of functions. They have their own professional association, CSA (Casting Society of America), and they're the primary gatekeepers. They perform a schizophrenic function: at one level, they defend the director and producer(s) from hordes of hungry actors storming the gates and looking for any crumb of recognition, any job, at any price. At another level, the casting director's job consists of combing through the universe of performers and having knowledge of an incomprehensible number of actors who work in a broad spectrum of styles: comedy, tragedy, melodrama, character study, musicals, intimate sketch and improvisational comedy, dance—everything, including commercials and short experimental films. A good casting director can break down a script and be able to provide a list of actors for every part, a mini-menu of available and qualified talent.

All the tools of modern digital technology are employed, both by actors and those who would employ actors: online videos, websites, blogs, electronic submissions—anything that gets the name, face, and voice of individuals to the directors and producers. In collaboration with the director, the casting person or agency prepares the *breakdown*, a short summary of all the available parts, with a brief character description for each role. A breakdown service then disseminates lists from multiple production companies to a select list of paying subscribers, actors, agents, and managers. A subset of additional specialized companies have their own subscription lists, but in essence, everyone is selling access to a centralized list of what's available. Depending on their financial resources, actors can maintain paid subscriptions to all the breakdown services, buy one and trade for others, or obtain unauthorized copies any way they can.

Once upon a time, actors spent hours getting photographs, reproducing them, typing resumes, attaching the two, and physically circulating them to anyone in the casting process: agents, managers, studios, production companies, ad agencies, and independent casting agents. They also had to assemble a reel composed of clips of their work, and circulate that unwieldy piece of film or videotape to the talent bookers and buyers. In the present digitized world, actors can maintain a presence on a website that has their work available to be viewed at a click. Eight-by-ten-inch glossy photos are rarely circulated, but every actor has a few in the trunk of his or her car, along with a DVD or a flash drive with his or her representative work, "just in case." As for the novice or beginner without a body of work to show, he or she will eventually find work, one way or another, or quit the business. Theater, film, and television present a peculiar professional choice: one chooses to find employment in a shrinking universe of rare opportunities, and "success" is managing to earn enough money to qualify for pension and health coverage in one of the performers' unions. In all of film, television, and commercials, there are approximately 3,500 to 5,000 unique acting jobs annually (including series regulars, hair models, and announcer voices). There are more than 120,000 union actors trying to get those parts, and untold millions of wannabes who think it would be cool to be on TV in *any* capacity—either in competitive quiz or talent shows; in reality shows (a dozen thirty-somethings locked in a house or on an island); or in an assortment of documentaries that focus on extreme jobs (ice road truckers, lumberjacks, and Alaskan fishermen). There are also onscreen opportunities for borderline psychopaths: hoarders, prisoners, the morbidly obese, dysfunctional families, self-destructive "extreme sports," and people who will expose themselves whenever and wherever a light goes on and a camera turns and, even more surprisingly, sign a release form that permits unlimited exploitation of those images.

Trained or not, ready or not, union or not, there is no way to discourage the permanent parade of those who want to be in the public spotlight at any cost. If you are one of these, you'd be well advised to do something to learn your craft: take classes, interact with a community of like-minded would-be performers, and take any menial or intern job that lifts you a millimeter above the surging, renewable crowd around you.

Since reality shows have their own aesthetic, they shy away from "casting," which implies that the subjects are not "pure" amateurs; hence the term *talent coordinator* for someone who lines up the exhibitionists and aspiring performers for their fifteen minutes of fame. Let it be noted that more than one legitimate acting career has begun in this primeval swamp of ego-driven performance and simple narcissism. A willingness to be observed at one's unguarded best or worst can lead to popular stardom.

Most importantly, the director and producer work closely with their casting representative. He or she offers input and suggestions, and then initiates contact with the artists or their managers and agents, makes offers, and negotiates basic contracts. Stars and multimillion-dollar contract negotiations are usually delegated to producers or business affairs lawyers or, in the case of an independent film, the entertainment industry law professional who is handling all the work on the production.

A casting director may bring in a hundred actors for a single part, if time and budget permit. Or more commonly, he or she may narrow the choice to three or four finalists, who are presented to the director either on film or in person, and who may read selected scenes in a conventional audition process. That process is simple: the responsible executives (director, producer) and the casting director sit in an office or rehearsal space, and successive actors (or teams of actors) perform a short scene from the film or series; this may be recorded for playback and comparison later. At the end of the day, based on what they've seen, the director and other responsible executives make a choice; usually, the director has the final word. As a director, you will have to exercise your arbitrary authority carefully; if there's someone you absolutely can't stand or stand to work with, say no. If there's someone you feel is *perfect* for the part, fight to include him or her in your cast.

All in all, judgment, tact, instinct, experience, and relationships are all essential components of casting and crew selection. Statistically, over your lifetime you will have a few perfect teams and a few wretched, frustrating, incompetent crews. For the most part, by being careful and following your instincts, you should have a pleasant experience that will result in lasting friendships, long-term working relationships, or both.

CHAPTER 4

What Kind of Director
or Boss Are You?

Over the years, the Directors Guild of America (DGA) has raised objections to longstanding terms of art and job descriptions such as *casting director*, *director of photography*, *art director*, and *fight director*. The DGA never succeeded in overcoming common industry practice and terminology that predated the formation of the union. Back then the Directors Guild's goal was obvious: since there was only one director to a film, other job titles with *director* in them were at best misleading and at worst eroded the authority of the director who was the sole "captain of the ship." By now it is no longer an issue; the director is generally recognized as the sole commander-in-chief of a project that is in production, and his or her authority is rarely questioned. He or she may report to a producer, but with a few production department exceptions (AD and unit manager), the director is the boss. Because one can become a director without much previous experience, it would serve the company well if the boss understood, accepted, and exercised his or her authority with some degree of wisdom and compassion. Whether you are a god-king like James Cameron, presiding over a $300 million collaboration; or a novice with a pitch in her pocket, a digital camera, friends on call, and a vision of a two-minute video, your responsibilities are the same:

- Understand the project.

- Appreciate the project.

- Devote your full attention for as long as it takes to make the project. This is also referred to as *commitment. Commit* to the work.

- Be completely open and prepared to deal with the unexpected.

- Maintain a constant clear and personal vision of the project in its entirety.

- Accept the changes that must be made, and execute them in a way that does the least harm to the totality.

- Lead by example. Never be seen to be doubtful, wavering, or unsure of yourself (there will be times when you are all three, but it does the company no good to be made aware of the fact that you are uncertain). If you are floundering, flounder with grace and apparent purpose. In short, the rule is "never let 'em see you sweat."

It would be easy to leave you with these rules, but it would be cruel to do that without at least a hint at how put them into play, so we'll expand on the list:

Understand the project. This means that you have read or written or collaborated on a text that is pleasing to you. A story, poem, script, concept, painting, insight—it doesn't matter where the thought began, only that it now exists as a script waiting to be made. Understand it as a literary work that has a style of its own, maybe a genre piece, a slice-of-life, a vignette—all the way up to a three-hour, full-blown epic adventure. This means complete familiarity with the plot and characters, and the ability to discuss any aspect of the production with your collaborators and provide them with direction that is consistent with your insight and understanding. Do *not* think that you can do this by combining a few pat phrases such as "It's *Die Hard* in a submarine" and "A musical in which *Girls Gone Wild* are intergalactic zombies."

Appreciate the project. You can understand a thing completely and still not like it. It is of immeasurable help when you love and understand something enough to devote some period of your life toward realizing a vision. If you love it enough to do it, your innate appreciation of the material will translate and inform your collaborators. Your excitement will buoy them up, and they will serve you well not only as working partners but as friends, teammates, and employees who don't want to disappoint you. It's usually not possible to maintain unalloyed affection for something 100 percent of the time, but try to stay in love with the project for as long as you're doing it. It also helps in post-production, marketing, and publicity to have visible enthusiasm for your work. This may be the origin of the old movie maxim:

"In Hollywood sincerity is very important; once you can fake that, you have it made." This is not to say that unconditional love is necessary for every project. It is one of the hallmarks of the true professional journeyman/craftsman that he or she can deliver a flawless, well-executed, and moving film simply by "doing the work." Keep in mind that this level of professionalism usually comes only after years of hard work and experience.

Devote your full attention for as long as it takes to make the project. Commit to it. This seems obvious, but in creative work, there is no substitute for focus and concentration. Ego has no home there, and worrying about image and appearance will usually distract from the job at hand. Never stop paying attention. If there is a lull in the production, you can think about the work that is yet to begin, the work you have already done, and how it all integrates with the work you are doing. You can't look bad if you are doing your job. It rarely helps to be overly analytical and judgmental of the work as you are doing it; if you've planned properly and understand what you are doing, the work will take care of itself. "Commitment" is a flexible concept, and somewhat mystical. You are devoting your entire being to the realization of an abstract work, a concept or a script that has no real-world existence beyond the written page or mental image. The challenge is to differentiate between what is possible, what is probable, and what is impossible. The cliché "Nothing is impossible" may work for self-help books and self-actualization seminars, but for the foreseeable future, unassisted human flight *is impossible*. You can dream about it, but you can't really fly. Ever. Don't try, you'll hurt yourself. Now go back to work.

This bright-line distinction between the impossible, the improbable, and the possible is much more difficult when dealing with the abstracts of production, but it's wise to remember there is a time to yield to reality (there are only so many hours of daylight to shoot) and a time to hold onto your commitment (changes to the script or shooting schedule *are possible*.) It may be a utopian ideal, but *there cannot be commitment without clarity.* Art thrives on ego and narcissism, but when they interfere with good judgment, they must be put aside. Commitment will help you climb a mountain; clarity will keep you from jumping off a cliff.

Be completely open and prepared to deal with the unexpected. The great Prussian military strategist Carl von Clausczwitz said, "The most careful plans disappear in the fog of battle." Which is to say, we are not in absolute control of anything. A film is a collaboration of a million pieces that can go wrong, and when production begins, the battle is joined. Murphy's Law suggests: "If something can go wrong, it will." Experienced production managers and directors intuitively understand that Murphy was an optimist. Any production is a stew of egos, ambitions, desires, and defenses. For reasons as simple as a sticky electrical switch or an actor's suppressed Oedipal rage, things can and will deviate from the script and the production plans. When these problems can be resolved with a retake or a five-minute break, they should be. If the remedy is complex and perhaps even

unfathomable, it is still up to the director to do something—
take a break for milk and cookies, make a phone call to the
actor's agent, have a quiet conversation with a grumpy cinematographer, or call out a careless stagehand. Most problems
can be fixed, either on the spot or after some period of reflection
and study. As the boss, you are responsible for choosing your
tools to deal with the problem. Try to be wise and thoughtful, or
at least be seen as understanding. Let the tool be in proportion
to the job: a dropped coffee cup is not a reason to call a halt to
production and yell at Mr. Clumsy. A missed cue that blows a
lengthy setup and adds a day to the schedule is reason enough
for a lengthy sit-down-and-shout after the rest of the day's work
is done. And finally, a simple tantrum and barked arbitrary
demand can sometimes clear the air and allow the production to
proceed. If the black hat fits, put it on. Even the most skillful
jockey may use the whip in the final stretch. "Just do it" and
"Because I say so" are sometimes the appropriate tools for the
job. Like all good tools, the authoritarian voice can grow hoarse
and ineffective when it's overused.

**Maintain a constant, clear, and personal vision of the project
in its entirety.** In a collaborative endeavor, every partner is
generally most interested in his or her part of the vision. It is
your job to bring it all together. Your partners can't be faulted
for this; you are relying on them to bring the full range of their
specialized experience to the assignment. You don't want your
lead actors worrying about where to store props, or the caterer
to be concerned about lighting the set. Keep the departments

focused on their individual assigned responsibilities. There are only four people on the set who must pay constant attention and be aware of all things at all times. They are the director, the cinematographer, the unit manager/AD, and the script supervisor. They are respectively the brain, the eyes, the body, and the memory of the production.

Lead by example. Despite the fact that only a few key personnel pay attention to everything all the time, it is also true that the entire company looks to the boss for leadership and inspiration. This is evidenced by something as simple as the dress code on the set. If a director wears a suit and tie every day, the entire company will be slightly more formal in their wear (excluding those departments like grip, electrical, and laborers whose clothes must be practical). If the director favors baseball caps and jackets, you can expect the department heads to repeat the theme. Although this is trivial, it points up the deep psychological need for the company to feel a unity of purpose and identify with a leader. Since the director is usually that person, almost all behaviors will be affected by the company's perception. A terse, laconic style of speech may prompt a similar language in the crew, and excitable enthusiasm for small details will provoke similar responses from others. Part of the director's isolation is the knowledge that there are times when you will have to suppress your fear, anxiety, and uncertainly and present the illusion of clarity and purpose...Be an actor (but not as a regular habit—cast and crew will catch on, and a disillusioned company is not an effective unit).

A cast and crew, like any pack or herd, will follow the leader. If you are that leader, you owe it to them not to run headlong off a dock, plunge into a swamp, or wander aimlessly in circles. Act as if the path ahead is clearly marked, and don't break stride as you head in the direction you think you should be going.. The good thing about a pack or herd is that they will protect your back and flanks, and the wiser members may even point out pitfalls and dangers for you to avoid. A cohesive unit working with informed leadership can accomplish near-miracles. Nothing in your personal behavior or temperament should give rise to doubt and fear in the company; directors have to wear their authority easily. PS: Nobody's perfect (surprise!) You may falter, stumble, and occasionally think you appear ridiculous. As a result, you may notice the company floundering a little and witness a few minor breakdowns in the chain of command. At times like this, it is best to remember the prominent World War II British poster found in London bomb shelters during the Blitz, which said, "Stay calm; carry on." If it worked in the Battle of Britain, it can work for you. Rest assured you will usually find your footing soon enough and be back on the right path.

Accept the changes that must be made and execute them in a way that does the least harm to the totality. Again, it's the same for a one-day short film, improvisation, and a sixteen-week mega-studio production. Someone or something will go wrong, malfunction, or simply be forgotten. Nothing in your bag of tricks has prepared you for this eventuality, it is beyond the experience of your most senior staff, and a replacement part is thousands of miles away. The temptation is to raise a commotion, assign blame, and demand an explanation. These behaviors may be useful for venting frustration, but they don't solve the problem. It is here that people turn to the director with that look that says, "You're getting the big bucks, tell us what to do." We are not of the school that believes that any decision is better then no decision. Of course, if bullets are headed your way, it's a good idea to drop down. After that, like any good soldier, take a moment to figure out where the fire is coming from and where to find cover. Once out of out of harm's way, figure out if you are going to shoot back, attack, or retreat. There is no dishonor in using your rational mind and raw instincts to help you come to a decision, and there is always a decision possible. Remember, a decision to defer a solution is not a decision. The problem remains until it is solved. The solution can be short term (just enough to get you through the day's work), and in most cases, this is the preferable choice. Why? Because it allows all departments time to recover, regroup, and come up with alternatives. Haste is the enemy. An ill-considered decision may create more problems than it solves, and there are no extra points for solving problems that don't exist. Just fix or replace what is broken, and work around the gap, and remember tomorrow is another day. *It also helps to know that great things can be accomplished if you don't care who gets the credit.* Accept help and consider the suggestions of all your collaborators—they may have solutions that will surprise and delight you. Finally, it is calming to remember that anything that can happen to you has probably happened before to somebody else, and most of them survived and prospered. Those who didn't make it compare the experience to a parachute that fails to open: a classic "Oh, shit" moment. An epitaph that reads, "He (or she) didn't see it coming."

Lead by example. Never be seen to be doubtful, wavering, or unsure of yourself—in short, never let 'em see you sweat. This not to suggest that you attempt to project an aura of invincibility and aloofness. Leave that to Alexander the Great and John Ford. Everyone knows you put your pants on one leg at a time, and if you're cut, you bleed. We've spoken about the isolation of the director, and it is rarely lonelier then when a baffled or bewildered crew is looking to you for their next move. At times like these, you can simply say, "Give me a minute to think about that," and walk two steps away to establish a bubble in which you can concentrate undisturbed. At other times, if there is a natural opportunity for a break, take it. You and your principal collaborators can use the time for analysis and determining options. Only in sports is there a penalty for "delay of game."

On a big studio film, time and money are considerable factors, but even then, no director was ever replaced for taking some time to solve a problem effectively. There will come a time when a problem is so large that it defies easy handling—for example, the death or injury of a principal player; a natural catastrophe; a massive technical malfunction; or acts of God, such as wind, weather, earthquake, volcano, or tsunami. In these situations, your first obligation is to protect human life and your second is to preserve the material you've already shot. After that, think about replacing equipment, moving to higher ground, or fleeing the country. Remember, in the early days of filmmaking, agents of the Motion Picture Patents Trust would disable cameras with gunfire. Things have calmed down since then.

Everybody has his or her own way of dealing with problems and directing others. As we've seen from the preceding, there are mechanisms for the process, but the way in which those mechanisms are employed will define your personality as director. Most authority figures fall into either of two categories: shouters and talkers. Each has its own virtues and flaws. Shouters speak loudly and authoritatively and in simple declarative sentences, often in the imperative. Like the sea captain, field officer, or drill sergeant, they speak so as to be never misunderstood and certainly not disobeyed. Obviously this works better in the military and in other life-threatening situations where actions must be completed quickly and efficiently for the survival of the company. Although the analogy of a movie set to a battlefield or a ship at sea is accurate in some respects, it would be silly to expect people to blindly follow orders on a set as if their lives were at stake. Nevertheless, the exercise of command in this hard style is an efficient way to move large numbers of people and huge amounts of material. It's no accident that photos of directors at work in the early days of film show them speaking into megaphones to amplify their speech.

Talkers, on the other hand, speak more quietly, may use more complicated sentence structure, and may address their remarks to much smaller groups. If a talker is dealing with a large crew or big set, he or she will leave the shouting and the bullhorns to his or her AD. Talkers are no less authoritative as directors, and there should be no misunderstanding as to their intention to command. All directors have to maintain control of the set and the actors, and command the respect and obedience of the crew. This may sound like a seminar in leadership; it is. A director leads by example, by inspiration, through intimidation, through fear, or through any judicious combination of those elements. It's best in life, as in directing, to have some knowledge of yourself and your persona. Contradictions in leadership styles tend to confuse your collaborators and your crew and will hamper the work. If you are normally soft-spoken and rely on persuasion and empathy to achieve your goals, you don't have the grit to be a shouter. Of course you can teach yourself to bellow and bluster, but for most people, it won't ring true, and any group will see through the charade and lose respect for your authority. On the other hand, if you have a background in sports or have been a natural, loud leader in your peer group, you may be a born shouter.

Contrary to the assertions of some misguided authoritarians, people are not sheep and will resent being herded by a barking dog. This is especially true of actors and the film crew, who have come to their place in the world through the cultivation of difficult skills and the mastery of subtle emotional truth. They will consciously or unconsciously quickly see through most poseurs. It is easiest if your style of direction is an extension of your lifetime skill set. There are loud, arrogant bullies with the soul of a sensitive shy "artiste," and there are quiet, rational-speaking leaders in whom beats the heart of a raging gorilla. They are rare. It's a cliché, but it never hurts to "be yourself."

Unfortunately, there seems to be a human tendency to form ranks around assertive personalities whether they know what they are doing or not. Many soldiers have been led to their deaths and many shoddy films have been made, all because of leaders who substituted bravura for brains and impulse for logic. Because of the innate respect most actors and crews give to directors, a loud bad apple can foul the whole barrel. Don't be one of those. There are also directors who are neither shouters nor talkers. They may be naturally uncomfortable in large groups; they may be obsessed with an internal vision they have difficulty sharing; or like many beginners, they may just be unwilling to speak up and take charge when they themselves are troubled by indecision or unsolved problems. Let's call them thinkers. If you are one of these (as a beginner or outsider), please understand that thinkers are perfectly capable of making frequent good decisions, they can analyze situations properly, and they have the ability to talk to actors about what they expect or require of a performance. The only mistake is to fail to communicate.

Shouters, talkers, and thinkers must all be able to tell a crew what they want, ask actors to modify their performances, and in all ways take responsibility for guiding a collaborative project to completion.

There are a variety of tools to make the job of realizing the script run more easily. These include the following:

✓ checklists (like this)
✓ posting outline note cards on a corkboard or white board
✓ storyboards
✓ posting visuals (cast and location photos)
✓ dictating notes on the go
✓ diagrammatic aids

Recent advances in management theory have highlighted the importance of checklists in many fields of endeavor. Originally designed for airplane pilots, checklists have become indispensable in managing hospital infection rates and completing large construction projects. The checklist is simply a way of managing a host of details that are so complex that it is difficult, if not impossible, for one person to remember all the details and correct sequences. A director's checklist might include such things as:

✓ everything necessary to a particular location
✓ a discussion with an actor about the nuances of the scene and development of the character
✓ a list of all the visuals that are special to and necessary for the project from start to finish

Similar to the checklist is the process of making outline notes. These can be jottings on $3" \times 5"$ cards pinned to a corkboard or lists made on a whiteboard. It is a flexible way to present a lot of information in a visual field that can be quickly understood. Notes on a board can be contemplated in solitude or viewed by a group in order to share information quickly. The board exists in its own individual space and can be referred to by everyone on a need-to-know basis. It is also a useful way to spot conflicts and inconsistencies before they become logistical problems. Short notes on a board can also be a repository for jokes and ideas to be incorporated into the production. If it's worth remembering, it's worth writing down.

Storyboards are like the panels of a graphic novel or comic strip. They can be elaborately drawn by professional illustrators who specialize in creating visual renderings of the script, or they can be simple stick figures with arrows showing camera movement and action within the frame. Whether they're artistic works that stand on their own or simple scribblings in the margin of a script, storyboards are a way of planning a sequence of shots without requiring a DP or crew on a set. There are gifted storyboard artists who can create a sequence of drawings that embody fluidity and give a sense of movement in still frames. Storyboards are most often used in commercials; animation; large-budget, effects-driven films; and extended action sequences where it is imperative to visualize the sequences before filming them.

Posting visuals of cast and locations is similar to storyboards, except you are using real people and actual places as aids to your memory. Sometimes the juxtaposition of actors' photos will clarify the relationships between them. It is also helpful to see photos of the actors in makeup and costume. Sometimes the examination and study of photographs will lead to new insights into the character or new development for the story. Panoramic photos and collage techniques can illuminate the physical locations where the film is going to be shot.

Dictating notes on the go can be done with a cell phone recorder, a pocket recording device, or any means of voice capture and playback. Thoughts can be recorded as they occur and transcribed later, either as postings to the bulletin board or action memos to the production crew. Notes can be dictated at the end of the day as a journal, and used to plan the next day's work. It's useful to begin each dictated note with a recipient and a subject, much like a short informal memo, text, or email. Notes can be reviewed in private and erased, or transcribed for further study and distribution. A collection of notes can easily become a personal journal or serve as the basis for a larger literary work.

The most common diagram for a director is a time line, which can often become a scroll with a literal line upon which are inscribed the actions and events of the story. A simple example:

TIMELINE: "GOLDILOCKS & THE THREE BEARS"

DAY 1: MORNING	MID-MORNING	MID-DAY	AFTERNOON	
				→ END
|	|	|	|	
CREDITS				
9:00 a.m.	9:30 a.m.	10:00 a.m.	1:00 p.m.	
Goldilocks goes for a walk	She finds a house in the woods, decides to enter it.	After tasting porridge and testing beds, she takes a nap in the littlest bed.	The three bears return from their outing, discover something's wrong.	

Other helpful diagrams are:

- A table of organization that visually describes the production crew hierarchy.
- A cast of characters with relationship lines, indicating how they relate to each other; perhaps a family tree for the cast, if it's a historical drama spanning time.

If an outline is to be read by anyone else, it must be clear, complete, and cogent. *Never show anyone unfinished or incoherent outline material.* It causes problems, creates misunderstanding, and confuses the writing process. Showing anyone a rough or unfinished outline will only make your life much harder than it already is.

CHAPTER 5

Writers and Writing

The director doesn't work in a vacuum; the only one lucky enough to start from nothing is the writer. As in Genesis, first comes the formless void, and then, in the beginning, there was "The Word." There is a constant creative tension between writers and directors in film and television. In the world of theatrical motion pictures, the director is the primary authority figure. In episodic series television, the writer-producer (or "show runner") is the god-king, and the director is more of a hired hand. The reasons for this are as complicated as film and television history, but it is a reality that should be accepted as we move on.

Unless it's a camcorder shooting "reality," or a self-actualized YouTube or web video quickie made on the fly, every project has some initial text that is the basis of the story. That text may be as simple as the one-page outlines that were used to make silent movies or as complicated as the 200-page screenplay for an effects-driven major motion picture. Most commonly, the screenplay is a unique document that has evolved over a century of filmmaking. It has conventions borrowed from theater and is unique to the studio film.

Tabs and spacing to differentiate between dialog and stage direction are formally prescribed; there are even software programs specifically dedicated to writing for the screen. Teleplays and screenplays differ slightly from each other but are generally similar, and most everything that any director will be asked to direct will be in that conventional format.

In the European filmmaking community, a movie often begins as a filmmaker or director's original concept. The director then selects a collaborative partner (usually a writer) to render that concept as a film script. The production proceeds with the active collaboration between the director and writer until it's a completed film; that process makes it easier to understand the French preoccupation with the "auteur" concept. The literal translation of auteur is the English word "author," and all that implies. In the American model, which was developed during the era of major movie studios, writers were contract employees, engaged to do original work or adaptation by a studio/employer who would then assign or hire a director to realize the finished script. There was little collaboration between the elements. They were all employees of the central authority (the studio). The studio would then assign a contract producer as overall supervisor and, utilizing employees across the spectrum of production, generate the finished film ready to be exhibited in the theaters that owned the studios.

Network and cable television is the last vestige of the studio system, in that a supervising producer, who is usually the creator of the show or a close collaborator, oversees every script from inception to broadcast episodes. That person is someone who literally "runs the show," which explains the job title and description: "show runner."

Most writers wish for a model contract based on that between the playwright and the stage producer (most commonly known as the Dramatist Guild Class A Production Contract). This is a contract model that gives the writer absolute ownership of and authority over his or her written words. Like a novelist's publishing contract, it specifies the terms under which the work is licensed for a production (never sold). Every production pays a royalty to the writer, and no production may tamper with, alter, abridge or expand upon the text. Like the novelist or songwriter, the playwright of a live stage productions is the uncontested owner of the words.

Due to the complexity and demands of modern production, these absolute rules have become eroded by time and circumstance. The concept that no word can be changed without the playwright's consent has fallen victim to the demands of the producing organization, endowment funding, and the exigencies of the tryout, the workshop, and the test-audience process. In theater, a subclass of meddler/ "creative executive," also called the dramaturge ("drama-turd") has evolved as an often unwelcome partner in the creative process.

The raw material for all directors and actors is the text, whether it is a screenplay, a teleplay, a stage play, or notes for improvisation. *The text is not a "blueprint."* This is a common analogy, but incorrect. A blueprint is a schematic scale-diagram that indicates how materials are put together to create a three-dimensional, solid object or structure. It's not a thing, it's a picture of a thing; and anyone who can read a blueprint can build the object. It will turn out the same anywhere in the world it can be built.

A script, on the other hand, is more than an image; it's the raw material from which the thing is made. It's the foundation, frame, and structure of the project. Think of words as gold, diamonds, iron, or oil. They can be shiny, pliable, sturdy, or slick. The words are the basic elements of performance, and they inform the scenery, music, pictures, characters, illusions, lighting, costume, hair, and makeup of the finished product. In the literal sense, the writer's words are the narrative and dialog that are the root of the audience's experience, and a script is a thing that exists in its own right. Give that script to ten different filmmakers in as many different countries, and you will get ten different movies that may or may not even resemble each other.

Please understand this in your soul before you start changing the lines around to suit yourself. The words didn't fall out of a dictionary onto a page, nor were they selected by a computer's random process. A writer selected each one for its specific linguistic meaning—its cadence, sound, or tempo—and positioned it in a string of other words for a purpose. Words are the atoms of the script universe, and when you smash an atom, you risk a chain reaction that can destroy that universe. As writer Charlie Hauck said, "Ideas abound, everybody has them. It's the damn words that cause all the problems. You have to pick the right ones and put them in the proper order."

Until the time when all beings communicate with perfect telepathic understanding, we have to rely on words to convey the more complex concepts. Evolution has given us language; it's a mistake to ignore it.

Don't panic; under certain circumstances it is okay to change dialog and edit text.

It happens all the time, sometimes for a good reason and occasionally to good effect. But understanding the primacy of text allows you to approach editing a script with the proper respect and understanding that every change has consequences, both known and unintended.

Writers are happiest when no one changes anything and the script still works. Directors are happiest when the script just works, however it's been changed. Actors are happiest when they have a lot of words to say. Satisfying these competing interests is the most demanding part of the collaborative process.

Directors and bosses, in their desire for the production to move smoothly and comprehensibly, are motivated to adjust dialog and occasionally reorganize plot elements for the purposes of "making the story work."

Writers must be flexible enough to agree to make adjustments to the "sacred text" when a story point is foggy or dialog appears forced, flat, or unnatural. Actors will make changes so that dialog "feels more natural to them," because they have memorized it incorrectly, or because they feel the character needs "something more."

Actors: *There is no such thing as "My character wouldn't say that."* If the words on the page are not mixed up by mechanical error, they are what your character would say. Those words are the dialog on the page as written and approved by the writer, director, and producer. *It's your job to make them work.*

Note to writers and directors: you will be continually astonished by the actor's ability to take dialog that appears flat on the page and make sense of it and make it real. That is the unquantifiable genius of the actor's art—to take carefully crafted, scripted text and speak it in a way that makes it appear to be spontaneous, natural human speech.

If an actor has issues with the dialog or the character, the time to resolve those problems is at the first reading, during the rehearsal process, or privately with the appropriate creative authority. Let us repeat: "Creative authority" is different in every production. In series television, it's the executive producer/writer. In feature films, it's the director. In the theater, it's the director and the playwright, and in an improvisation, it's a fluid concept that depends on how the particular improvisation is staged and the degree of autonomy given to the company by its boss or director.

The final and unarguable creative authority is the audience. It is their perception of your efforts that will recognize and validate what you have done. In live theater, the feedback is immediate and actually controls the pace and intensity of the performance. In film and television, you can only look at the playback of the recorded image with the audience to judge its effectiveness. On the Internet, audience response is evolving, depending on such considerations as real-time feedback loops and other esoteric technical gadgetry. There are also those illuminating and irritating comments that viewers will reflexively post in response to anything they've seen.

A few words about "the audience": In the 1953 Rodgers and Hammerstein backstage musical *Me and Juliet*, a stage manager sings a song to a nervous ingénue, describing the audience as a "big, black giant" with a thousand eyes and ears that's different every night. The audience has been a part of the performance equation since the dawn of theater, and for good reason. A group of humans watching an event brings a collective intelligence to the experience that exceeds any individual's personal capacity for understanding.

We can look forward to a time when exhibition media can interact with live audiences to make prerecorded audiovisual material more responsive and interactive. Imagine a comedy film that can hold for a laugh, or a drama in which the emotional intensity of an actor's performance and the editing of the scene(s) can change, as some future technology "reads" an audience's response and adjusts the performances accordingly! Until the day that perfect feedback loop arrives, we are stuck with the archaic process known as "writing." Here are some observations and instructions on that art:

Notes on the Writing Process

Writing requires a depressing amount of time. The time's not necessarily spent in the physical act of setting words on paper (or typing them into a word processor), because typing isn't writing. The time spent "writing" must exclude or limit any activity not related to the creative process. That may mean sitting in a room waiting for inspiration or impetus; or watching movies and television for clues as to how to solve problems you may be having; or reviewing research material and notes, looking for that significant detail or bit of information that illuminates a scene, or helps you make sense of the story.

Organizing a flow of ideas; putting dialog in character's mouths; determining the sequence of events; figuring out what happens, where and when it happens, and to whom and how it happens—that's writing, and it means that most of what you do must be somehow focused on that job. There will be times when you're definitely not writing, and it's best to recognize those times and not worry about being away from your script during them. Sleeping in, partying, a night out, a vicious argument, a romantic interlude, a road trip, a beer run, a visit to a jail or hospital, a trip home to see the family, a ball game, playing sports—you may think these are times when you're not writing, but you may find that what you see and hear and smell along the way is exactly the detail you need for your story. *Write it down! Make a note!* You'll find much that is relevant in your own experience, as well as much that is distracting.

In short, living is writing, and writers spend only part of their creative time in the physical act of writing. Much of what you do just walking around through life, half-dazed, is writing . . . it's the half that's not dazed that's observing, remembering, analyzing, diagnosing, correlating, interpolating, and so forth. If you can use what you see, and learn from what you feel, your experience becomes reliable research.

There's a temptation for writers to maintain a distance from direct experience, in the name of objective observation. Christopher Isherwood wrote a collection of short stories called *Goodbye to Berlin* in 1930. It was source material for a film (*I Am a Camera*) which morphed into a Broadway musical and a musical film (*Cabaret*). The famous opening lines of the anthology begin with the words, "I am a camera with its shutter open, quite passive, recording, not thinking," which sums up the "unengaged" approach to writing. It's far less fun than active involvement.

It's possible to write well about ships and sailing from research, but we believe you learn more in an afternoon at sea than in a month of reading Melville and watching the America's Cup on television. On the other hand, when writing action/drama, let's agree that research and reasoning-by-analogy is preferable to the personal experience of robbery, murder, and arson, either as perpetrator or victim.

In the collaborative work of filmmaking, the writer of an original work stands first, and alone. You often work in a vacuum, creating something out of nothing. You are pouring a foundation in a vacant lot. On that foundation is erected either a monumental cathedral of a film or a jerry-built shack of a potboiler movie or hack sitcom.

What follows are one author's subjective observations on what goes into "professional screenwriting." It's based on personal experience writing for money in most of the literary forms in which writers earn a living, and on a practical level, it reduces the art of writing to a trade or craft, the mechanics of which can be learned, codified, and reduced to fundamental principles. Screenwriting is a literary craft, like journalism or technical writing. In its highest form, it transcends craft and becomes art, and at any level of accomplishment, it's a specialized literary form that combines storytelling, description of visual elements, and the ability to create plausible dialog between human beings, which is an art in itself (ask any playwright).

Some of what follows may be dreary and obvious, and it may repeat ad nauseum what every other writing text in a saturated market says. Fine. Just skip it. Here's what's important:

The mechanical act of writing requires concentration, and concentration requires a certain single-minded purposefulness. That means a conscious effort to limit distraction. Marcel Proust wrote in a cork-lined room to eliminate the distracting sounds of the outside world. Writers who can afford studios make them single-purpose workplaces, dedicated to the process; a home office in which you write checks for the rent is not a "writer's studio." Neither is a kitchen table on which a meal is being prepared, served, or cleaned up. Nor is any residence in which television, audio equipment, video games, or substance abuse are in obvious use, even if only by others. Write alone, in any place where you can limit or control distraction and focus on the job.

There are two ways to write, and two kinds of writers: regular and sporadic. This goes for students as well as employed or unemployed professionals. "Regular writers" set aside a period of time every day for the actual work of putting words in sequence, using whatever technology is comfortable or workable (pencil, pen, typewriter, voice recorder, desktop, laptop, dictation). Just like a factory worker punching a time clock or a student attending class religiously, the regular writer starts on time, limits his or her breaks, and concludes after a suitable work period. It can be a four-, five-, or six-day week, but significant time is spent writing, every day. This is an efficient and productive way of writing, and it's a way to accomplish a great deal in a limited amount of time. For example: five script pages a day is not a difficult goal, and on this schedule, a screenplay can be written in a matter of weeks.

How much time should you spend writing, per day? For the professional, whose sole occupation is writing, it's been suggested by more than one source that the optimum time to spend at a keyboard is roughly six hours in any waking period. This seems to be common experience. More than six hours of continuous writing is usually fatiguing, and the quality of the work seem to diminish by hour eight. Less than six hours can be productive, but there's a sense that more could have been accomplished if the work had continued. Students who face multiple demands on their time, and must satisfy course requirements across a wide spectrum, have a more difficult time of it, and the six-hour figure is probably unrealistic.[1] This holds true for sporadic writers as well, even though their work patterns are completely different.

---

[1] It's not unrealistic to achieve a six-hour stretch during a weekend, on Saturday and/or Sunday, when attending classes or lectures is not a factor.

"Sporadic writers" work in spurts, alternating days and nights of fierce activity with days or weeks of avoidance behavior, distraction, and inattention. For the sporadic writer, the process of writing is best described as making a series of ever-decreasing concentric circles around the keyboard until there's nothing left to do but write, since all other distractions have already been explored. Sporadic writers like to work against deadlines and within limits, since only the fear of missing a deadline or failing a course provides the incentive to work.[2]

Then there's a writing method that transcends the others, and may be experienced by both regular and sporadic writers. It's something common to artists, athletes, religious mystics, and the occasional politician. It's been described as "peak experience," "divine ecstasy," or "being in the zone." It's an altered state of consciousness, achieved without drugs, during which normal perception of time is suspended.

In this exalted state, physical limitations seem to disappear or become inconsequential. The work becomes effortless, words come easily, the story tells itself, and characters assume a life of their own, practically dictating dialog that flows naturally and easily onto the page. If and when that experience occurs to you, encourage it, do nothing to impede it, go with it, and write until you can't continue. Then simply stop, and take some time off before resuming work. (Usually one sleep period is enough, whether it's a day or a long nap later.)

---

[2] For the employed writer, compensation is usually tied to completion, so the economic incentive is substantial.

The work done in this ecstatic mode may not be perfect; be prepared for diversionary flights, overdetailed narrative and stage direction, and redundant dialog. Not to worry---cutting and editing come later. The important thing is to take advantage of a remarkable creative state that doesn't occur too often in nature. Some of you may regularly create in this mode; others may experience it rarely, if at all. It's included here because its extraordinary nature requires recognition.

A Cautionary Note

The creative state (practically a "writing frenzy") described above can be artificially achieved in a number of creative ways, most commonly through sleep deprivation or by chemically altering consciousness ("working high"). Be very wary of work done in an altered state of consciousness.

Under the best of circumstances, words written this way are likely to require sober and meticulous editing. Under the worst of circumstances, work done in an altered state can be useless drivel, an embarrassment to yourself and to the reader.

Summing Up

Whether you're writing sporadically or regularly, ecstatically or prosaically, the work must be done. Concentrate and exclude distractions. Set aside time to write. Look to your outline as the overview of your screenplay. It's the model, sketch, and working drawing of the job at hand. In it should be the solutions to your problems. Concentration will produce results, and the results will be work of which you can be proud. The achievement of the writer is the script, which exists independent in time, concrete and specific. A script is not a film, but no film exists without a script.

CHAPTER 6

Understanding Economics

The macroeconomics of motion picture and television financing are beyond the scope of this book. Nevertheless, some familiarity with the financial aspect of production is necessary for every director. It's no accident that the Director's Guild of America includes in its standard director's contract a provision that requires the director to "sign off" on a production budget. That is because the day-to-day working conditions of the director will be inevitably shaped by the budget, which dictates the amount of time, money, and resources allocated to the day's work. In shorts and student films, budgets are less formal ("How little can we shoot this for?"), but they still set limits on what can be accomplished.

The art of breaking down and budgeting a screenplay of any length is an arcane task that requires actual production experience, familiarity with dozens of union contracts, and a sixth sense for anticipating the unexpected. Every project begins with a text (The Script). The second unavoidable step in the process is

The Budget, which is based on The Script. Most filmmakers with limited hands-on production experience will probably wind up paying to have a budget prepared. Everything that follows lives and dies in direct relationship to how it fits or breaks the budget.

Another reason a credible budget is necessary is that financing sources need numbers: how much a picture will actually cost is of utmost importance to investors who hope to profit from the project. Even the legendary rich uncle or sympathetic grandparents want to know what the hard dollar hit on their savings is going to be. Obviously if a project's funding is guaranteed, the budget will not undergo the same sharp scrutiny by people who actually care if an investment is returned. Even if a project is cooperatively financed by a variety of small investors and out of the pockets of the creative talents involved, the budget will dictate the priorities of the production (e.g., if there is no money allocated for set construction, it can be assumed that shooting will be done on real locations).

A professional approach to budgeting even the shortest film is an absolute necessity and art form. Any project larger than a sixty-second YouTube video made on a webcam or shot on your cell phone requires a budget. It is important to understand that one of the iron laws of finances is that you can get 95 percent of a project finished for only 50 percent of the cost. It's that last 5 percent that will drive you crazy, because as much money as you have already spent, you will have to find again to complete your vision. (There is some flexibility in the exact percentages, but there will always be a surprising amount of money that is needed "just when you thought you were done.")

The other inflexible and immutable budgeting consideration is the "two out of three rule." Every seasoned production manager has sat down with his director and drawn a variation of this diagrammatic equation called:

GOOD-CHEAP-FAST

"You can have any two," says the Production Manager, "but all three are impossible."

- **You can shoot it fast and good but it won't be cheap.**
- **You can shoot it cheap and fast but it won't be good.**
- **You can shoot it good and cheap but it won't be fast.**

Determining priorities is vital to the production process, and the "two out of three" equation can be applied in different ways to different situations, depending on things such as wind and weather, the location, the actors, the complexity of the photography, and the thousand unforeseeable accidents in every department of the production. A good boss will be constantly juggling all of these elements while at the same time trying to preserve your ultimate vision and the collaborative view of what the project actually is. Curiously, it is sometimes easier to find funding than it is to budget the funds you find. Financing for any project can be as simple as reaching into your own pocket for cash and credit cards; and then, in ascending levels of complexity, these are scenarios you might employ:

- Internal cooperative financing ("let's all chip in").
- External informal financing (friends and family chip in).
- External formal financing (backers from any source commit funds in exchange for ownership and revenue participation).
- Production company financing (a backer or backers with exhibition or exploitation connections, someone with ties to exhibition).
- Direct financing (by existing distributors, studios and networks, nonprofit organizations, advertisers, and Internet sites).
- Multiple-source financing (a combination of commercial finance and distribution entities, plus cash advances from sales to territorial distributors and subdistributors).

Financing can be any combination of the above; everything beyond self-financing (spending only your personal cash) will require some formal documentation of the financial agreement. It may be as simple as a short letter of agreement informally summarizing the participants' duties and obligations, or as complex as a ponderous financing-and-distribution agreement that can run over a hundred pages. It's true that some deals have been concluded over drinks and memorialized on a damp cocktail napkin, but a hundred years of filmmaking have produced "definitions of profits" that are as complicated as any medieval or Talmudic analysis, and less fun to read. In brief, all contracts should include the following (another checklist!):

- ✓ the amount being offered
- ✓ the expectation of delivery
- ✓ a schedule of payments
- ✓ a return on the investment
- ✓ a specific equity or ownership position to the financier (if that's being offered)
- ✓ the assignability of positions
- ✓ the liability for completion financing
- ✓ insurance for errors and omissions
- ✓ approval of a budget
- ✓ provision for arbitrations of disputes
- ✓ place, date, and time of the agreement
- ✓ references to all other necessary documentation

Unless you're Bialystock and Bloom (the lead characters in Mel Brooks's *The Producers*), you can't give away or promise your backers more than 100 percent of the revenues. The definitions of production expenses, negative cost, and classification of income are all minefields for the novice filmmaker. Seek professional help for the contracts; some entertainment lawyers will exchange their services for a percentage. There is no economy to hiring legal counsel that is not specifically and verifiably experienced in entertainment transactional law, because nothing in the curriculum of a conventional law school or an ordinary law practice will include the exceptions, swindles, assumptions, and "customs and practice of the industry" that are common to film and television services agreements (contracts). The simplest financing and distribution agreement is an invitation to downright chicanery, phrased in double-talk polished by masters for over a century.

Here are the terms and phrases that are unique to show business, and a potential trap for naïve or careless talent:

Property (or the Property): Not a piece of real estate; this is the script or treatment or synopsis, book or short story, or anything that is the project at hand. A screenplay is a property, as is the finished film—from the term *intellectual property*, which is used to define such things as copyrights and trademarks (unlike *real property*, which refers to land with boundaries and property lines on which you can walk or build a fence or a house). Intellectual property is a way of defining ownership of musical, literary, and audio-visual works, and is being stretched to accommodate other intangible concepts, such as choreography and staging. Traditional copyright holders object to extending intellectual property protection to these related interpretive crafts. The concept of intellectual property is peculiar to Western European law and custom, and is foreign to Asia and East India, which may explain, in part, the acceptance and extension of piracy (theft) of audio-visual product without royalty and reuse payment. As of this writing, the practice exists in China and much of the rest of the world, both east of Suez and in any marketplace on the planet where goods are bought and sold.

Pitch: As a noun, *a pitch* is a verbal-shorthand presentation of the property, which may vary in length and intensity but is usually how the project is described in advance. As a verb, *to pitch* is to verbally sell or describe the property to another. The legendary two-word pitch that sold the television series *Miami Vice* was this: "MTV Cops." Got it. Let's move on.

Back End: This refers to deferred compensation, usually in the form of bonuses and percentages, a "participation" in the ongoing revenue income stream that results from the exploitation and sales, rentals, and other exhibitions of audio-visual product (or property). Back ends can be net of expense, "after recoupment" of "negative cost" (what it actually took to make the picture), "participation from first dollar gross," or some combination of all of the above.

The Gross: This is an incomprehensibly difficult concept to grasp, but it begins with the fact that the "grosses" that are reported in the press as a picture's earnings (usually in its first weekend) bear little relationship to the actual income that flows to the film's producers and distributors from the exhibitors who own the theaters. The term of art that describes real income is "rentals," which is the sum that leaves the box office in Peoria and eventually arrives in Hollywood. The gross never includes all the money the audience pays for popcorn and soda, which stays in the hands of the theater owner and is never shared. There are many forms of gross: producer's gross, distributor's gross, gross before participations . . . ad infinitum.

The Net: What a project earns after everything permissible is deducted from the gross. Often referred to as "monkey points," a percentage of net profits can be extremely lucrative in certain situations, usually when there is a reasonable budget to be recouped; there are no gross profit participants; the distribution deals are straightforward; and deductions for marketing, prints, and advertising are controlled and strictly audited.

Residuals and Royalties: Deferred compensation for after-market and "ancillary" use of intellectual property or performance rights; the subject of intense negotiation, bitter invective, corporate greed and anxiety, and international disputes over treaties and conventions. The concept of "monetizing" the reuse of intellectual property in the new Internet technological age is fluid and evolving; no textbook currently available describes the global situation accurately, and the global situation itself is indescribable and difficult to quantify. American and Canadian artists have some protection from their union contracts—which mandate fixed residual and reuse payments—but these slices of the pie are subject to constant arbitration, litigation, and renegotiation, and as of the current writing are still evolving, usually to the detriment of the artist.

Approval: Not to be confused with consultation, which is a meaningless term thrown into a contract as a sop to someone's ego. You can be "consulted," give a forceful opinion, and demand a change, but once someone has said, "Whaddya think?" and you've given your answer, the "consultation" clause in your contract has been fulfilled: there's no obligation for anyone to act on your opinion. Approval, on the other hand, is an explicit requirement that needs an affirmative confirmation (of the script, locations, budget—whatever). Beware of actors' contracts that give them approval of the director or script—the writer's and director's jobs depend on their good will. On the other hand, if you're an actor, you may want to include approvals in your contract to make sure (as much as possible) that your career won't be in the hands of a nincompoop or fool. There are plenty of those on both sides of the camera.

By now it's obvious that the actual business part of "show business" is as unique as the profession itself, and filled with dense contracts full of verbiage, boilerplate, and multiple appendices that are the result of more than a century of misunderstandings, mistakes, exploitation, and secret agendas. As stated earlier, a simple law degree is only the beginning for understanding and analyzing show business contracts. Outside of a few specialized elective courses taught by law schools in Los Angles and New York, the subject is usually not in the curriculum or on the bar exam.

Readers here will learn the basics in either of two ways: through the painful process of trial and error, or by building early and permanent relationships with a community of related or like-minded professionals. Knowledge is usually gained through experience, or by paying the price (and accepting the advice) of seasoned, qualified professional counsel or mentors.

Or be like the grasshopper, and enjoy the fleeting rewards of the moment and leave the financial planning to the ants, who will inherit the planet (and the movies) when we're done with them.

CHAPTER 7

Commercials and Short Films (The Thirty-Second Exception to Every Rule)

There once was a Golden Age when talent could count on big paydays and access to the latest technology and the opportunity to work with gifted if not famous actors and musicians. It was the era of the first music videos and big-budget commercials for network television. All of the techniques described in other chapters were used by directors, writers, and actors during that era, and they can still be helpful.

However, there is one important difference. In the music video, the artist and his or her management dictate the contents, and in the big-budget commercial, the sponsor and the ad agency are the ultimate authority. If a musical artiste thinks a camera angle is unflattering, then trust us when we say that the director will never get a chance to use that angle, and even if he or she talks the artist into allowing the shot, it will be cut in postproduction. In music videos, the artiste is the boss.

In commercials, the star, the focus, and the center of all attention is the product. Bosses may be working with glamorous models, authority figures, or sports stars—and will have to get a charming, convincing, winning performance out of them—but that performance has only one purpose . . . to sell the product. In commercials, the product is the boss, and since the boss is an inarticulate detergent, automobile, insurance policy, or some other thing that's not a person (despite the clever voice and animation), the filmmaker will have to look elsewhere for direction and instruction.

The director who is working hard with a performer to achieve a desired effect can't lose sight of the fact that it's a sales pitch, pure and simple. Even those heart-catching institutional commercials for a telephone company, or the sentimental appeals of people with a grave medical condition, are still about "calling home" or "Ask your doctor about. . . ." Yes, you will have to coax a convincing performance out of the players, but the lasting impression you must leave is that it is a good idea to use the phone or buy a pill.

As of this writing, the network airing of a national commercial is still the only way to get a commercial message to tens of millions of buyers. As a result, the budgets for creating these messages are proportionately huge. It is not unusual to spend seven figures on a thirty-second commercial and its variants. If feature films were shot with this cost/time ratio, every movie would cost hundreds of millions of dollars. Because the economic stakes are so high, even the most talented and respected directors are relegated to the role of a journeyman contract director in the old studio system—that is, a replaceable cog in a well-oiled machine.

For actors, the ability to read commercial copy is an absolute requirement to any entry-level employment in today's world. Every agent and manager will demand that the actor have an understanding of the different types of commercials and how to perform them. The categories are as follows:

- **The Talking Head:** Close-up of an actor/spokesperson directly addressing the viewer.

- **The Character:** A spokesperson identified with the product, such as the Maytag Repairman.

- **The Product-Driven Spot:** In which the actor is there only to serve the product: to drive the car, drink the beer, brush the teeth.

- **The Celebrity Commercial:** In which the principal actor is someone recognizable in the public arena: an actor, athlete, astronaut, model, or famous musician.

- **The Celebrity Voiceover:** A recognizable voice is heard, not seen, selling the product.

- **Voicing an Inanimate Object, Cartoon Character, or Animal** (the Geico Gecko, Scrubbing Bubbles, Morris the Cat, the Bacon-Loving Dog).

- **The Infomercial:** A long-form program that mimics the talk show format but is all about a single product, such as a juicer, fitness equipment, a hair product, or a get-rich-quick plan.

- **Industrial:** Any of the above, produced in-house for the employees of a company or other organization as a learning tool. (Formerly known as training films.)

- **"Real People":** People with little training as actors are used to play themselves in a representational situation. ("Mom, Dad, and the kids"; theatergoer; pranked or punked victim.

- **Body Parts:** Hands, hair, eyes, feet, and teeth (and maybe other body parts) are used for their own visual appeal, usually employing specialized models.

If a director is new or just beginning in this arena, he or she should be prepared for both the perks and the pains of shooting a product. In addition to the normal executives, producers, marketing geniuses, and financiers one finds on a movie set, there is a whole other level of management imposing executive decisions. They go by many names: creative director, art director, copy chief, account executive, product supervisor, media buyer, media manager... the list goes on. Essentially this management level represents the agency or intermediary who facilitates (or blocks) effective communication between the manufacturer of the product and the creative elements in production. Call them "The Client."

More than in most workplace situations, the director must be adept at determining pecking order, chain-of-command, and when to politic and persuade. In commercials the director can't simply say, "Because I said so." Like all rules, you can break this one, but be prepared for the consequences. You might be a "maverick genius"—or more likely, out of work.

For one thing, the dialog is sacrosanct. Every syllable, cadence, and punctuation point has been studied, reviewed, approved by management, and even tested or previewed in a focus group. It is "set in stone." Even if an improvised line or an actor's transposition of dialog is an artistic improvement, chances are you'll be criticized for permitting it. If you're lucky, there will be someone in authority on the set who will take the responsibility for approving the change; but don't count on it, and don't waste time on retakes of the unapproved version. If it's that good, the client will recognize it in postproduction.

On the next page is a chart to help guide you through the world of commercials.

Essential Element, Films & Television	Essential Element, Commercials	The Director's Obligation	The Actor's Task
Interesting characters, as created by the writer.	Idealized, attractive models; or typical "real people," whichever is demanded by the client.	Defer to the client's casting choices, or make irresistible suggestions for "someone different."	Conform to the client's notion of who or what you are—no more, no less. Don't embellish; be prepared to speak faster or slower on command. If you claim a skill (riding, surfing, playing a musical instrument), *be sure you have it.*
Spend the time to get the best performance from all the actors.	Light and shoot the product perfectly, then everything else.	The product is the only star in the production.	Never upstage the product, and be clear about who you're talking to and what you want from them or what you want them to do for you (usually, to buy the product).
Scenery, locations, and sets that serve the story.	Scenery or setting in which the product looks best.	Exotic, spectacular locations, or the latest CGI visual-effects techniques.	Be prepared to go anywhere, or pretend you're somewhere else while acting in front of an effects screen.

CHAPTER 8

Defend Yourself:
Physical and Mental Challenges
Facing the Director, Writer,
Actor, and Producer

The Physical

Production is strenuous physical work. It's no accident the classic advice to new directors is "Get comfortable shoes." The fancy chair with your name on it will be largely unoccupied because you'll be on your feet: talking to other members of the production team, working on sets and locations, and perhaps pacing nervously (out of sight of the others—remember to never let them see you sweat). If you're the writer on a feature film, you may not even have access to the set; if you're a show runner, you own the set. In either case, prepare for the same challenges. It is also no accident that the director and principal actors are subject to a physical examination for insurance. It costs the company time and money when the key personnel are not working at optimal physical capacity. It also costs the company when the director or producer set a poor example; no matter how valuable it may seem to bond after the shooting day is over, a night out with cast, crew, producers, writers, backers, or locals will cost you more in hangover and recovery time than you will gain in loyalty or on the "good guy" scale.

Shooting time is the most expensive time in a production. On a feature film, a delay of minutes translates into a loss of thousands of dollars. No unnecessary delay can be tolerated. As an example, consider the situation of the first AD on a water location. The company was relying on local boat owners to ferry the cast in their personal boats to and from the set. A unpredictable change of the wind caused a local's boat to start smashing into the dock. The owner asked the AD if they could hold up shooting while he moved his boat. The AD said, "Absolutely not, I'm not stopping shooting to move a boat." The owner protested, "It's going to wreck my boat!" The AD replied, " We'll buy you another boat." It was cheaper for the AD to replace the craft then it was to stop shooting for the length of time it would take to move it. The boat owner never understood this, and yet the lesson is clear. Writers have a delicate balance to maintain. If a quick change or correction will fix a problem, speak up. If an actor or the director has a question about the text, answer briefly and concisely (usually through the director). A few well-chosen words can fix a host of editorial and production problems, which is why writers *should* be on the sets of the productions they've scripted. So stay healthy.

Because time is a precious, perishable commodity, pre-planning your self-care is extremely important. When production starts, you won't have time to consider your diet, sleep patterns, exercise, emotional health, and mental acuity. It's best to build these positive habits before going into a production when everyone else's problems become your own. In commercial, large-budget productions, there is usually someone with medical training on the set; in low-budget and no-budget productions, you'll be lucky if someone can slip you an aspirin or a bite to eat. Be aware that there are liability and insurance issues when handing out or taking medications.

If you run, swim, jog, or do any kind of aerobic activity, make sure you allow yourself some time to maintain your cardio-vascular fitness level. If you have sufficient lead time before diving into production, consider increasing your levels and efforts when working out so that once on the set, you can endure the inevitable time shortage. Alfred Hitchcock and John Huston both were directing into their eighties, and each one coped differently: Huston, who had emphysema, needed oxygen and was required by the insurance company to have a stand-by director in event of his incapacity or death. Hitchcock, who was overweight, rarely left his chair and directed everything while seated close to the camera. Both men conserved every bit of energy for their primary task.

Because one of the seductive experiences of becoming a director is becoming god-king on the set, the new director may think it is his or her due. Actually, one of the harsher realities is that because a director is indispensable, every effort will be made by every department to keep the director happy, healthy, and functional to whatever degree the budget permits. For your own well-being, you may have to turn down the more tempting offers of assistance: "Another drink?" "Another pillow?" "Another donut?" "Another painkiller/upper/downer?" "More sexual favors?" Know when to say no.

Another point about diet and nutrition: it's common to gain or lose weight while directing a production, either from reflexive gobbling of easily available comfort foods, or failure to drink or eat enough to maintain a balanced diet to keep yourself at your normal body weight, assuming your body weight is normal to begin with. It's common to get so involved in the production that you "forget to eat," which may be good for dieters but not for directors.

Without delving into food faddism or the vegan-versus-meat debate, be mindful that carbohydrates elevate blood sugar, protein slows the absorption of carbohydrates, and both are essential to a balanced diet. Low blood sugar can get in the way of clear thinking, and most food excesses affect health and mental activity unfavorably. Part of your preparation will be to determine what your optimal diet for energy, endurance, and mental clarity is. Then, stick to that plan as much as you possibly can. It should be noted that the all-in-one "breakfast burrito" served on most locations may actually be a healthy start to a long day. The combination of bacon, eggs, cheese, salsa, and sour cream on a tortilla may be disagreeable to the conscientious healthy eater. However, it's a carbohydrate and protein combination that's more solid than a protein shake, although some favor beginning the day with a properly mixed liquid blend of the essentials.

Sadly, the "craft service table" on most studio productions and its low-budget equivalent is usually loaded with items of questionable nutritional value: licorice whips, salted nuts, pretzels, chips, and candy bars of all sizes. As a rule, beware of anything you can take by the handful.

A recent trend led by stars and the occasional thoughtful director has been to provide sound nutritional snack foods: fruits, salads, vegetables, and organic snacks. Beware, again, of anything you can eat by the handful, although some combinations of raw nuts, raisins, and dried cranberries are acceptable.

The Mental

The source of most drama outside of the script is the actors, and anywhere they congregate may be a hotbed of intrigue, gossip, and disinformation. This is also true of anyone who talks to actors, so view the makeup, hairdressing, wardrobe, and transportation departments as minefields. Even on a low-/no-budget production, where all the departments are combined in the person(s) of your overworked colleagues, a few misplaced or ill-chosen words will resonate throughout the production, and anything said in confidence is public knowledge as soon as it can be repeated. A favor for one will be expected by all, and any violation of boundaries will result in the loss of those limits.

This is not to say a director cannot speak or be spoken to; if that were true, directors would be the loneliest people on the set. Feel free to chat about wind and weather, but remember that in all close-knit male groups, from nineteenth-century British colonial armies to the crews of nuclear submarines, there are three topics deliberately ignored: women, politics, and religion. In a less gender-specific world, include members of the opposite sex as subjects to be avoided. Add to those topics these sources of friction: the problems of the production, the character of the personnel, and the personal lives of everyone on or near the set. The director's problems are uniquely off limits; like the captain of a ship or the leader of a combat patrol, his or her thoughts must remain private. We discussed the director's isolation before; it goes with the job, it even has a name: "the loneliness of command." If you must share gossip and commentary, do it with someone far from the set or the production: a therapist, a life partner, a close family member, or an animal companion (these may all be the same individual). If you're a writer, your closest confidante may be the director. If he or she is not sympathetic, the same limits apply to your options.

A strategy (or habit) that many executives (including directors) find useful is to acquire or maintain a group of friends or confidantes with whom you can share frankly and safely. The advantage of this is that the natural loneliness of command is softened by a close-knit circle of advisors, sounding boards, and lieutenants who can be trusted to keep people and things organized and functional (including yourself, on the bad days). But, beware—the inherent danger is that your group becomes a "posse," a gang that gives the appearance of a support group but is, in fact, a barrier. These individuals are people whose principal interest is preserving their turf, influencing your

decisions, and insulating you from all criticism and useful input.
They become gatekeepers and relish the role. How can you tell
the difference between a small circle of friends and a posse
that's a clique and a claque? A quick checklist is in order, again.
They're not your faithful friends and confidantes if:

- ✓ The only people close to you are on the payroll. If
  that's the case, you're buying loyalty, not earning it.
  Think about it: A person has the choice of telling you
  what you need to know and losing his or her job, or
  misinforming you and staying employed. Which do
  you think will be most useful to you? (Think Elvis,
  Michael Jackson, and the like.)
- ✓ You learn crucial information from outsiders who
  tried to get to you directly but were diverted.
- ✓ Other old friends complain about your inaccessibility.
- ✓ Items shared in your circle become public knowledge
  or gossip, or wind up in the tabloids (if you're newsworthy).

And speaking of being newsworthy, if you've achieved a
level of success that includes managers and agents, be aware
that they have other clients and "relationships" with employers
and studios, and unless you're their only client, there are other
people they have to "service" (an inelegant word for what they
do). Agents and managers may certainly have professional and
business goals that are not in your best interests, although they
will never tell you, and they may actively dissemble (lie) to

you about their reasons. They can also function as an effective firewall, an impenetrable barrier between you and everyone else. If you are fortunate enough to have this level of professional management, always be aware that firewalls can keep the good, as well as the bad, from reaching you. Which is why gossip is important.

When you hear (or overhear) gossip and criticism, *never* take it at face value. Confirm with secondary sources, check with colleagues, determine the truth as best you can, and immediately confront and resolve a negative situation before it undermines company discipline or hurts someone. For example, a director notices a cast or crew member is sometimes hard to find when needed. Someone observes that the missing person "must be taking a nap." "Why do you say that?" says the director. The answer: "Because whenever he's tired, he goes off the set, and when he comes back he's alert and talkative, bouncing around, ready for anything!" It's true that many people are energized by a short nap. It's also true that many people are energized by cocaine, crystal meth, prescription drugs, alcohol, or clandestine sex. It's best to resolve the situation with the minimum disruption to the company. (Which doesn't mean find more drugs or alcohol for the tired person—nothing disrupts a company more than the arrest of a principal.)

Of course, all of this will be gossip on the set the next day, but that's the way of the world. You have to get on with the day's work.

The same is true of less dramatic situations; the director and writer will be privy to the simple backbiting and competition, gossip, lover's spats, on-set location romances, and the sheer tedium and boredom of filmmaking. You will also be the subject of all of this chit-chat. Don't worry about it; leave "I wonder what they think of me" in high school, where it belongs. Although it's usually a matter of personal style, the director is best advised to remain enigmatic, above the fray, and focused on the work. Some directors, and others in the production, capitalize on fear and gossip, and employ them as tools in the manipulation and control of the company. We don't encourage it—not just on moral grounds, but because arbitrary inclusion or exclusion based on gossip makes people insecure, and insecure people usually don't function at their highest level, and that includes your valued posse.

It's also useful to remember that temporary personnel who rotate through a production (day players, guests, etc.) should be included as soon as possible in the company's routine and educated as to the expected standards of behavior. A cast and crew should be discouraged from harassing, hazing, or toying with a newcomer. Likewise, a powerful newcomer or the members of your inner circle should be discouraged from harassing or bullying any member of the production team for any reason. If someone needs to be counseled, disciplined, or fired, that's your job; don't delegate the hard decisions. (If it makes you feel bad or you want to remain forever "the good guy," you can ask someone else to do it, but it's not the strongest way to behave.)

Finally, a word about "The Suits." These are the elements of the production that are actually higher than the director on the chain of command: studio and network executives, financiers, ad agencies, and the producer who hired you. There are three ways to deal with them:

1. *Ignore them.* They have no idea of what you're actually doing.
2. *Listen to them carefully.* If they have some idea of what you're doing, you may make note of what their concerns are, nod and smile, and then ignore them. Or . . .
3. *Don't ignore them.* They may have genuine creative input that you will find useful. How is this possible? Many executives in genuine positions of authority (not just titles with the word *creative* in them) have long, hard-won experience that informs their opinions. Others may have come up through the ranks and shared similar issues as directors and producers; some may be artists-in-disguise, genuinely inspired by creative insight and inspiration; and some may be family members of the main money source.

Every situation will require its own carefully calibrated response. As a general rule, Suits are more helpful at your side than on your back. In the long run, no director benefits from having a reputation as being "difficult," and even huge commercial success doesn't insulate you from unemployment after a series of negative experiences and (God forbid) some commercial failures. For better or worse, continuing commercial success grants you license to indulge any and every creative impulse, makes you immune to all criticism, and excuses the worst excesses of personal and professional behavior. Despite all that, your principal motivation should remain your artistic vision, not vast wealth and immunity from prosecution.

All that said, every now and again, despite all your careful planning and the planning of your most skilled and trusted support team, things will turn sour, explode, collapse, or otherwise go from "all right" to "all wrong." The classic bumper sticker that describes this stressful situation is: "Sh*t Happens."

CHAPTER 9

When Things Go Seriously Wrong

The normal accidents and mishaps that can plague a production are predictable. Any experienced line producer, unit or production manager, or first AD will have a dozen solutions in her or his back pocket to cope with almost every known issue. There are "cover sets" (alternate interior locations) for days when bad weather shuts down a production. There are ways of photographing a scene to "shoot around" an actor who is incapacitated or otherwise not present. If there's a mismatch or an anachronism in a scene, an editor can work around it. The Internet has thousands of examples of errors and omissions that survived in the final release of films and television shows, such as wristwatches on Roman soldiers in a biblical epic, or air conditioners in the windows of turn-of-the-century New York.

There are usually ways to resolve almost every workaday production problem. Everyone who's ever done a day's shooting has a war story about mishaps and mistakes, or something that was overlooked by the cameraman or script supervisor and discovered only later, in postproduction. As we said in chapter 3, Hitchcock's advice, "It's only a movie," can carry you past the temporary emotional upset of small calamities. This is not about that. This is a short set of rules, and a few anecdotes, about how to cope with events that threaten to destroy, compromise, or invalidate your entire production or your vision. These events can be categorized as follows:

- Personnel problems (actors who go sick or missing, or even die in the middle of a production).
- Material or logistical failure (ships sink unexpectedly, buildings collapse, fires rage out of control, explosions are mistimed or too strong).
- "Acts of God," on a scale too large to anticipate (massive earthquakes, hurricanes, floods, tidal waves, forest fires).
- Acts of banditry, war, riot, piracy, or civil insurrection (as in any unstable country or lawless state, or by a criminal enterprise close to the production).

For a comprehensive list of terrible events, look at any homeowners' insurance policy for exceptions to coverage, read the fine print on a shipping invoice, listen to the disclaimers on television commercials for medical products, or (closer to home) consider all the elements of the standard "E&O" (errors and omissions) insurance policy on your own production (you shouldn't be shooting without one).

The most extreme case of personnel failure is the death of a principle actor during production after a great deal of footage establishing that actor has been shot. There are only a few ways to cope with this morbid eventuality. One is to replace the actor and reshoot the sequences in which he or she appeared with a new actor. This was done in the old studio days when Marilyn Monroe was too sick or unfit to perform in *Something's Got to Give*; she was replaced by Lee Remick. (Ms. Monroe died later that year.) More recently, Heath Ledger died during the filming of *The Imaginarium of Dr. Parnassus*, and three movie stars who were friends stepped in to fill out his role for director Terry Gilliam (Colin Farrell, Johnny Depp, and Jude Law).

The alternative is to integrate a replacement "double" into existing footage and scenes that have not yet been shot, which is what was done when martial artist Brandon Lee was shot on the set of *The Crow*. The producers decided to shoot around his footage using a double; despite the reluctance of the cast, the work was completed with a stunt man, and artfully reedited using existing scenes.

A less extreme personnel problem is the principle actor who is available for shooting but too incapacitated to function properly. In the early days of television, a famous syndicated series used an Academy Award–winning actor as the main character, who was in almost every scene. He was also famously drunk at this point in his career, and the long shooting days of low-budget television (they did thirty-nine episodes a season back then!) were too much for him to do sober. He managed to make it through most days, but a close look at the footage of that long-ago series shows several telltale signs of inventive coping by the director and crew.

Much of the actor's dialogue is fast-paced technical instructions spoken into a police-car radio microphone. Rather than risk repeated takes on the actor's close-up, the microphone is always positioned in front of his mouth, masking his lips, so that *all* the dialogue can be repeated at leisure in post-production—"dubbed" when the actor is sober and functional. In wider shots, when the actor is outdoors near his car, all the waist-high shots are cut off above the belt; crewmen often held the actor steady against the fender, out of the frame line.

The most original and creative solution to the problem of an actor who was falling-down drunk was to turn the floor into a wall. A file cabinet was laid on its side, bulletin boards and clocks were positioned on the floor to make it look as if it were a wall, and the actor was eased into position, comfortably lying down, one elbow on the file cabinet. Shot directly from above, the floor appears to be a wall, and the actor looks vertical, not horizontal. Problem solved!

In one of the author's personal experience with a troublesome mechanical shark in the original *Jaws*, a collaboration between the writer (Gottlieb) and director Steven Spielberg proved to be a blessing in disguise. For a variety of technical reasons, in a film made before modern computer graphics made *anything* possible, the repeated failure of the title player in the movie posed enormous logistical and budgetary problems. After months, every alternative dialog scene indoors, on land, and on board the fishing boat "Orca" would have been filmed. There would be nothing left to shoot if a solution to the problem of the absent shark wasn't found.

Since the script was still in progress during principle photography, it was possible to rewrite the story to accommodate the missing fish. The director's decision, implemented by the writer, was to make the shark more menacing by holding back "the reveal." It was possible to show the *effect* of the shark without showing the whole shark, or even its fabled jaws, for the first half of the film. Thus we saw the memorable opening death scene of a nude swimmer wracked by a huge unseen force, the sudden devouring of a kid on the beach, and a near-death experience of some hapless local fishermen who toss a rump roast on a hook into the ocean to tempt the great white. In each instance, nothing of the shark is seen, only the grim and deadly force it exerts on its victims. This use of an offscreen adversary builds the tension, and much of the drama and suspense of the movie is directly proportional to the anticipation of finally seeing the creature.

Jaws was lucky; it had a flexible script in an inflexible shooting environment. It was an expensive location, sets were built, permits and zoning were arranged, and the local citizenry was divided on the benefits of having a film company on location in their precious environment.* More often the script and story are locked, and the director has to improvise creatively to make up for life-threatening malfunctions, equipment failures, and drunk or dead actors. Look to the editor for postproduction

---

* For a complete discussion, see Carl Gottlieb, *The Jaws Log* (New York: Newmarket Press, 2012).

story, character, and dialog solutions, and to the CGI or optical houses for possible (and expensive) corrections to the flawed basic image.

As for acts of God, only prayer will suffice, and the sense to shut down and get out of the way when hurricanes blow, the waters rise, and earthquakes and avalanches disrupt the geography of your set.

Finally, since we live in troubled times, be extremely careful of locations. Usually, your insurance coverage or a nervous star or producer will guide you away from narco-states, kidnappers' havens, and places where you are vulnerable to pirates and bandits. Aside from the obvious (Somalia, certain Latin American states or countries, former Soviet Republics, and the Balkans), be wary and choose alternates; North Africa has countries that can (and do) stand in for much of the entire Arabic world, and there are places in the United States that have effectively replaced rural Mexico and wartime Vietnam. There are creative solutions everywhere for the resourceful director and his or her crew. *Avoid problems by avoiding problem areas,* and if your area becomes problematic, pack up and get out.

Otherwise, your most likely rescue will come from a Zen-like calm and an acceptance of things you cannot change; failing in the calmness and meditation departments, remember to have a good meal and a good night's sleep. And remember that annoying moppet Annie's musical advice: "Tomorrow's a day away," or Monty Python's lyrical chorus from The Life of Brian: "Always Look on the Bright Side of Life."

CHAPTER 10

On Actors and Acting

For the Actor

By now, if you are seriously interested in acting, you're probably tired of being talked about as an object or tool for producers and directors. Yours is a difficult profession, but there are opportunities everywhere; and as your work is seen by an ever-widening circle, you will find yourself examining a variety of employment opportunities, most of them unpaid. Outside of major cities with a vibrant local theater culture, your only chance may be in neighborhood or amateur theater companies—what is often called "little theater." In major production centers, such as New York, Los Angeles, Chicago, and Toronto, you may find yourself in "showcase" productions, put on by a company of actors wishing to have their work seen.

In Great Britain and Europe, there is a strong tradition of local and civic state-supported repertory theatres that can offer paid employment for actors—what was once known as "playing the provinces."

If you *need* to act, there's usually a way. If you need to make a living at acting and be a professional, you are best served by migrating to a production center. For most actors, the most gratifying part of the job is *getting* the job. You are already confident that you can portray the character; but being picked from a variety of competitors and being offered a contract or money or both to play a role, however small—those are the joys and highlights of your working life.

Sadly, of all the collaborators in the filmmaking process, the actor is the only one who depends on others to practice his or her craft; you can't "act alone." At the very least, you need other actors and a place to rehearse and perform any sort of production, even a one-character autobiographical monologue. Fortunately, work leads to more work, and with success comes additional opportunities for employment and an actual income as a professional actor. As noted earlier during the discussion of casting, there a literally millions of competitors, and the chances for success are miniscule. Therefore, it would be prudent to have a strategy for alternative income (or inherited wealth). The ideal is a job with flexible hours and an opportunity to audition and take a leave of absence when an acting job comes up.

Of all the collaborators in the filmmaking process, actors are the least understood. Unlike equipment or crew people, a malfunctioning actor can create chaos in a production. Worse yet, the levels on which actors can cause mischief are subtle, varied, and difficult to pinpoint. It's in your best interest, then, to train yourself in good habits. Many of these have been discussed earlier. All that has been said about defending yourself and maintaining your health on the set is especially important to actors. Unlike everyone else on the set, your art, your personality, and your physical body are all part of the character. In some acting schools, they talk about the actor's "instrument." You are your own violin: stay in tune, have all your bits and pieces ready, and be prepared to make great music when your entrance is cued.

With the collapse of the studio system decades ago, the concept of a unified style has fallen out of favor, and even during the golden age of the movies, each studio cultivated its own brand of acting. The training for young contract players would vary from studio to studio. An MGM ingénue was always slightly different from her sisters at Warner Brothers, Fox, and Paramount. Those days are gone forever; there are no "starlets," no contract players, no "earn while you learn" opportunities for actors. Nevertheless, the overall style of corporate filmmaking remains constant across the entire spectrum of soap operas, episodic television, network and cable programming, and independent and feature films, and as an actor you may expect to work in any or all of the above forms. Be aware that the challenges of the professions are increasing exponentially. Corporate employers are constantly squeezing the bottom line, and relentlessly exerting downward pressure on actors' wages and working conditions.

These days an actor has to behave like a business person: keep contracts, pay stubs, receipts for expenses, and all the records needed to substantiate claims for overtime, for pension and health coverage, and for state, local, and federal taxes. This is not optional, it's urgently important. Don't forget it when you get a job.

Before you get to that point, however, you need to be cast; in order to achieve that, you may have to audition, submit film of yourself, read for a part with a casting director or reader, and read just to camera. There are differences in the audition process for every type of production. What follows is taken from the authors' extensive experience.

As Toni Attell teaches it, there are many acting methods that can be used and that she teaches, but the "Attell Method" we'll present here is summarized as "Acting for Film, Television, and Commercials . . . Hollywood Style." Attell uses deepening relaxation exercises created from hypnosis to help students get rid of self-judgments, egos, fears, and phobias, and she helps actors instantly remember lines and build character. For example: If the writer has described a character as "an angry woman," it is the actor's job to fill in the blanks—why is she angry? This is called *back life*. What happened to the woman to make her depressed or angry? An actor can't just play "angry" all the time; there are many layers to acting, just as there are in real life. That's what you carry into the scene. You never just "say hello," you say "Hello" (or "Hi" or "Hey, you . . .") with a back life of what has just happened to you. That's what's called a "before moment." It can include the fictional weather, how you're feeling, how you got there, and your relationship(s) to the others in the scene. That's what you carry into the scene.

Creating Character: As an actor portraying a character, you'll want to know what you want from the other character(s) in the scene, or what you want them to do for you. These are called the *intentions*. Similarly, it's helpful to understand the *arc* of the character (where the part begins in its intentions, and how they change during the course of the scene). In addition, you'll want to figure out the history of the character. If you're lucky and it's a big part, many of the details will already be present in the text as dialogue and exposition; other details you will have to determine for yourself. For smaller parts that are not explored in the script or big roles where the history is left unsaid, the actor is advised to make choices. The director or show-runner may change, modify, or reject the actor's choice, but it's usually better to come in with choices made. Despite all this, there are actors whose process does not include backstory choices; they rely on appearance, behavior, and performance-in-the-moment to communicate all the audience needs to know. Certain iconic actors who bring a historic persona to the screen can rely on the audience's familiarity with their body of work to fill in the blanks in their character (more true in the old studio days for guys like John Wayne and Cary Grant and women like Bette Davis and Katherine Hepburn, and currently mostly for villains; Alan Rickman or Robert Englund ["Freddie Kruger"] leap to mind). In modern feature films, the bosses may actually play against type in casting villains and heroes, but in television, typecasting is endemic (as a rule; there are always quality exceptions when good work is being done).

Colors: Small, intangible sensory impressions that suggest the character's soul, spine, or core. Attell suggests that actors keep a journal of things that move them personally to incorporate into the work in creating a character: the smell of baking bread, the reactions of a cat being petted, the distaste of something spoiled in the refrigerator, a moonrise, a sunset—all the five senses leave impressions; usually picking two will help inform the character. Over time, the actor will learn which are useful and which will move a director to say "Don't do that." Keep what works, lose the rest, but always maintain the journal or its equivalent, and store those thoughts, impressions, and memories of moments for eventual use.

Secrets: Characters have secrets, things they never tell but hold onto for themselves. This goes beyond colors; it's actual character history and includes information that's not available to the other characters or actors—for example, Harry Potter's embarrassment at being raised by surrogate parents who never told him of his complicated past or gifts.

Obstacles: What is it that keeps the character from getting his or her desires fulfilled? Scripts are full of hints and direction in this area: unrequited love, secret admiration, friends who betray you, enemies who want to kill you, a teacher who doesn't believe in you, an uncaring spouse, a lover with a new partner—the list is endless. Life, like art, is full of obstacles.

The "Where": It's always important, Attell teaches, to know where you came from and where you are going, so that you keep continuity in the scene and in the life of the character. When you create a credible and absorbing environment, the audience is drawn into the scene and its natural sense of voyeurism is satisfied. Again, keeping a journal or script-specific notes is a useful technique.

Auditioning for Commercials: Most paid acting jobs start with an audition. Even unpaid work and student and short films may require a process of selection. Auditioning for commercials requires you to bring an attitude about the product. You always want to pick a positive attitude and not upstage the product; you *love* it and support its use. When looking at the camera, you'd best think of someone you know in order to bring a "light" into your eyes. This is important in all roles, but most crucial to commercials, during which you'll often be asked to address the viewer directly (through the camera). It's an old trick used by on-camera spokespersons, news commentators, television reporters, and program hosts. Don't just see an unblinking lens; look *through* it, and visualize the individual viewers watching you. The immediacy of television means you'll be speaking directly to them, as a trusted friend or kindly authority figure. In some cases (mattress and used-car commercials and certain infomercial product pitches), you'll be seen as an annoying but compelling stranger, the kind of person who grabs your attention on a street corner or carnival midway, and demonstrates a vegetable peeler or a juicer, an absorbent towel—anything that can be sold cheaply and fills a need. "This is something you need, want, and should have two of; send $14.95 *now* ..."

However, if you are working with someone else in the commercial, in a brief scene of some sort, make a relationship choice, decide how you feel about the person, how you love the product; keep that light in your eyes and that energy in your voice and body. Most commercials are only thirty seconds long; the dialog is generally inflexible and *must* be performed in the time allotted. The first few tries, you may worry about your lines and the time it takes to say them, but *trust your natural biological clock*, and soon you'll get it right. Always wear the outfit to the callback that you wore for the original audition. Keep track of this. Keep track of mileage, dry cleaning your personal wardrobe worn in production, coaching and performance classes. As we said, as an actor, you are also your own business, not only in commercials, but in every aspect of your performing career.

Slating: This term refers to when you identify yourself at the start of an audition film or tape. It's important to remember to smile when slating; directors, producers, and product and advertising types want positive people with visible self-esteem who can do the job quickly and correctly on their sets. Look at the camera, smile, turn side to side, and feel upbeat. Do not talk about traffic, parking, or any of the million negative things that may have happened to you on the way to the audition. (Note that you can always use those harsh thoughts to build a character; hang on to them for later.)

Auditioning for Film and Other Drama (or Comedy): When you audition, wear a suggestion of the character. If reading for daytime dramatic series television (soap operas), come as the character and play it all the way. Don't do small talk for soaps;

they need to see you and the character you have created. If you are auditioning for a feature-length film, take the time to ask questions of the assistant before you walk into the room with the producers. You don't want to make the casting director look bad. The casting team is on your side, they want you to get the job, it makes their job worthwhile, and easier. If you ask them a serious question in front of the bosses, it's embarrassing— you should have clarified all possible issues before presenting yourself to the room. Memorize your lines, and if there is a reader involved in the process (saying the other characters' script lines), really work with him or her. If there's only a camera, think of someone you know as being on the other side of the lens, and speak to that person, knowing what you want and why. Attell suggests that at that moment, you let go of all your preparation or rehearsal techniques; release your preconceptions, and your natural instrument will make the right choices. Whatever you do, don't hold back.

Auditioning for Television Series: It is important to hold onto the script pages (often called "sides") and occasionally glance at them once or twice so the director knows he or she can redirect you. You must still have the lines memorized, but look at the pages anyway—just to make sure you seem adaptable. If you are redirected, please listen, and just nod your head if you understand what changes are being requested. It will do no good to agree and then not change your performance; it's one of the signs of an inflexible actor. If someone is taking the time to direct you, take it as a good sign: they like you and are working with something they see and want in their show. Be prepared to take direction and remember it.

A Few Other Things to Remember: There is an unexplainable magic in the eyes and mouth. Remember: if your performance is projected in a movie theater, your face is sometimes two stories high, so less is more. If you have a lot of theater background, acting for film may be an unfamiliar style you need to practice. Keep it real, and remember it is the silence between the words that often conveys special meaning. You don't have to rush; just relax, respond, listen, look, and think about what you are saying. Sometimes not thinking and just responding is a reasonable choice, depending on what type of actor you are and what feels good or just "works." Keep it simple, make choices, let go of ego, *and let the character come through you, rather than trying to control the character.* This is also good advice for writers creating dialog for characters. Writers will often speak of a character "taking over," an odd moment of creative truth when the words the writer chooses seem to be dictated rather than thoughtfully crafted. It's the subconscious assuming creative control; don't fight it. You can always edit later.

Hitting Your Marks: Because of the uniquely technical nature of recording performance in any medium, camera angles and lighting can be crucial. When a scene is staged or rehearsed, in audition or on a working set, the position of the actor is noted by all the technical departments involved. In order to optimize the image, "marks" are placed as reference points. These are most commonly bits of colored tape on the floor to indicate where the toes of the actor should be; other times they may be a sandbag or some piece of set dressing, but in every case, it's a sign that screams at you to "stand right *here!*" If you miss your marks, you may be not lit as well; you may be blocking another actor or some important visual element or casting an unwelcome shadow. It's the sign of an untrained amateur to either miss the marks or be looking down for them. Be aware of them, pay close attention during rehearsal (it's all right to look down then), and then relax and let your body's kinesthetic senses take over. Trust you will instinctively find them, and you will. *As in all cases, the worst thing that can happen is that someone will yell "cut" and you'll have to do another take.* That's why they have numbers on slates! But don't make a habit out of missing marks; it's unprofessional.

Preparation is of vital importance to the actor. Never judge the character. Find all the good things about the character; layer him or her with all the good, likable, nonjudgmental choices; and let it flow. Attell suggests using the "Blah-Blah" method, first substituting the words of the writer with the nonsense syllables blah-blah-blah and then later adding some improvisation with the words in the text. Experiment with different intentions or objectives, or with your own words. Then, finally, bring it back to the writer's words as written in the script. Some actors think of words in their heads that relax them and help them understand the writer's text. Example: For the line "How are you?" the actor can *think* in his head, "Hey man..." and then *say* out loud,

"How are you?" (It'll sound quite different than if the internal starting text is "Excuse me. . . .") Directors and writers call these subliminal introductory words or sounds "handles," because they literally give the actor a grip on the speech that follows. It's generally not advisable to actually vocalize the handle, just *think* it.

A Note About Pre-Audition Rehearsal: All of the preceding tips and tricks for actors are to be used *in rehearsal only*. Once you have rehearsed your character and made your choices, go into any audition with all your choices already made, and when the reading or audition starts, forget any techniques and just let whatever happens just happen. A great technique for learning lines is to memorize four or five lines before going go to sleep and then add another four or five in the morning. Attell reminds the actor that the unconscious mind is most receptive in the morning and at night. That makes it the best time to make useful character choices. Later, by day, let it go and just be "in the moment." Using a bathroom mirror is a great way to rehearse, remembering to also say the other character's lines; in that way, you will have studied what the other character(s) in the scene might be thinking. It's also a useful technique for understanding the writers's overall intentions for the scene. Remember, these techniques are for preparation; during the actual process, listen and respond in the moment.

Auditioning for the camera: Most likely, a serious audition is recorded, either in a production space or at home for digital transmission. If you are asked to "look into the camera," don't play to a glass lens. Play to a mental image of a friend or a real person with whom you're acquainted, and perform as if you are in conversation with a human, not a machine.

In appendix A, you will find worksheets for the "Attell Method," which most actors will find useful additions to their study and preparation.

For Directors and Others

Actors, writers, and directors all use words differently. There's a vast vocabulary with overlapping definitions: *beats, intentions, objective, obstacles, arc, spine, backstory, secrets, underbelly,* and *core*—what the hell are these things? There's a glossary in the appendix that will help you, but be aware that there are great teachers and theorists who have all left a permanent imprint on the vocabulary of acting: Konstantin Stanislavsky, Uta Hagen, Lee Strasberg, William Ball, David Alexander, and the unrelated "Alexander Technique," Stella Adler, Michael Chekhov, Nina Foch, Robert Lewis, Herbert Berghof, and Sanford Meisner. Add to these the primary theorists of improvisation and television comedy: Viola Spolin, Paul Sills, Harvey Lembeck, and Del Close. The list and its complete exploration is beyond the scope of this workbook, but a simplified "unified" theory would divide acting into two basic dimensions: *interior* and *exterior*, or "from the inside out" and "from the outside in."

The exterior style is typified by classically trained British actors who spend years learning their craft employed on the stage in the classic repertory (Shakespeare, Moliere, Shaw) and in the BBC "white flannel" dramas that focus on British period pieces (*Masterpiece Theatre*). The epitome of the exterior (or "technical") actor was Lord Lawrence Olivier. It was said that when he played *Hamlet* on Broadway and had a hot date after the show, he could cut fifteen minutes from the running time of the play simply by speaking more quickly—with no loss of meaning, nuance, or poetry, just a conscious effort to "act faster." Many actors have unique and personal styles that generally begin with the externals: costume, location, props, accent, physicalization (a walk, a stance, etc.), a vocal mannerism, or specialized makeup.

The internalized style is generally credited for its origins to Stanislavsky, Strasberg, and the Method, typified for two generations by Marlon Brando, Shelly Winters, Paul Newman, and Joanne Woodward. Directors identified with the Method include Elia Kazan and Arthur Penn, and more recently, the British directors Mike Leigh and Anthony Minghella.

Directors, you should know, rarely identify with one style or the other. Thanks to the difficulties of casting and financing any film (studio or independent), a director should be capable of handling a variety of modalities and styles from his or her actors, blending the two into a unified style that is unique to the project. The successful fusion of multiple acting styles into a complete narrative is a primary goal, even a necessity, for any boss. Worldwide, there are hundreds of acting coaches and teachers, each with his or her own methodology and vocabulary. Every actor can pick and choose, even combine techniques. Actors should not try to remember or mimic technique in performance or auditions; the performance should be spontaneous .

In this regard, it may be a virtue sometimes to simply step away and let the actors work it out between themselves in rehearsal or even on the set. There are times when a director's heavy hand will inhibit the natural evolution of the actor's process. No director should surrender the set to the actors; overall supervision and approval is uniquely the director's primary responsibility. Never relinquish control, but never be seen as unnecessarily arbitrary or heavy-handed.

Because this is a workbook, here's a list of simple phrases for communicating with actors, regardless of their background or training (or the lack of it):

- "If you're not comfortable, I'm here to answer your questions." (NB: Be prepared to give a proper response!)

- "I'm open to suggestions, if they're appropriate."

- "If you want to try it completely your way, let me see it."

- "Please complete this sentence: 'At this point in the story, I am feeling _____ [actor supplies emotion], because _____ [actor supplies his or her motivation, objectives, backstory, intention, etc.].'"

- "Let's agree on the subtext [underbelly] of the speech or scene [every speech or scene has a subtext]; say it in your own words, expressing your own emotions, and then let's return to the text as written, and apply it."

- "Let's consider the 'Ws': Where are you, what do you want, why do you want it, what are you going to do to get it, who are you talking to, what is the relationship between the characters and what do you want them to do?" (NB: Usually all the answers are in the text, but sometimes they have to be inferred or deduced.)

- "If this helps you, try keeping a secret, or performing some action or activity that is rooted in the 'Ws' and supplements the script."

Seasoning counts, but experience makes things both simpler and more complicated; actors may have developed habits and routines that may conflict with the production process.

The greatest thing about actors is that they are constantly surprising. The surprise is usually an insight into character that the actor has found in his or her process. Some actors make careful notes throughout their scripts, and other actors may just jot down a few key words. But any actor who is serious about the craft is going to study the character in tremendous detail, without judging the character and without descending into a one-note performance.

For example: the best villains are portrayed by actors who stress the human qualities of the character (intelligence, obsession, compassion); these human dimensions make the character's villainy or crime that much more terrible or frightening. Good actors will also play multiple levels of character without apparent effort, so that we see all the complexity and variety with which the writer imbued the character.

Good actors—and by that we mean seasoned professionals who have demonstrated their ability and range in a variety of parts—may still need a director's overview and vision to guide them to a performance that serves not only their character but the entire story. Sometimes that means spending a lot of time with the actor, either in individual rehearsal or simply in one-to-one conversation. Other times the director is best served by staying out of the actor's emotional path and concentrating on the other aspects of the scene, such as visual composition, staging, and so forth. One of the director's primary functions is to coordinate the inner action between actors so that the performances add up to a cohesive whole; an overly broad performance might be brought down, while an overly introspective performance might be made more outgoing. Even in an isolated monolog or one-person show, no actor is performing in a vacuum. Theater, film, television, and new media are all collaborative enterprises; no one works alone.

New technology is enabling performers to work more and more as independent entities. Webcasts and podcasts are often made without directors, but almost every human effort requires a feedback loop. In the absence of a director, the opinion of someone you trust or another professional (such as an editor) can be useful. If the suggestions make sense, modify the performance accordingly.

In all other forums, actors, regardless of their level of experience, must accept the director as the primary source of objective comment or opinion. The director must understand that his or her opinion means nothing without the respect of the actor. Actors are not subordinates; they are equals in the collaborative process.

One of the most important suggestions the director can give while guiding the actor is to commit to the role. Earlier, we discussed the importance of clarity to commitment; but in the case of the actor, who is dealing almost entirely with subjective creative choices, a complete commitment may require a degree of involvement that may seem to be uncaring or egoistic. However, it is precisely this kind of immersion that some (not all) actors require in order to do their jobs in the best way possible. The director may have to rein in an overly committed actor whose behavior is so out of control as to be frightening or threatening to the company, or even physically dangerous. Similarly, any boss has to be mindful of an actor's sudden withdrawal into an impenetrable shell, in which the "circle of concentration" is disturbingly similar to low-functioning autism. Usually things won't reach these extremes, but like the Boy Scouts, "Be prepared."

It's a common flaw of many directors to confuse the title with the responsibility. The title is a rank in the hierarchy of production, and the director may be first among equals; but arbitrary, willful, or uninformed choices can erode the respect and eventually cause mutiny and dissension. The deadliest sign of impending disaster is when crew or actors stop offering any suggestions and say, "Just tell me what to do."

The stage or the set is not an open forum. The tired analogy that the director is the captain of the ship must be tempered by the fact that even ships' captains take pilots to steer them through unfamiliar waters, sail their ships where their owners tell them to go, and don't attempt to run the engines and steer the ship unassisted. Trust the actors to do their homework in the same depth as the property master and the cinematographer. Although the acting craft is subtle and personal and sometimes incomprehensible, every actor brings his or her passion for the character to the set. Their involvement shouldn't be discounted or ignored. They have probably thought more about their part than most bosses have.

The actor's involvement with the role may also be an impediment to the collaborative process, especially if the actor has spent more time in the profession than the director. While the actor's obsession with the role may blind him or her to the larger picture, the director must always keep in mind the totality of the story. When this happens, the actor must be gently nudged back in the direction of a collaborative role, and possibly even a subordinate place.

A director must sense the areas where actors are afraid to go, and help lead them there. The words and phrases a director uses in these circumstances should encourage actors to use their common sense and innate experience with human behavior—for example, "Please give me more energy [volume, intensity, involvement, excitement] in your delivery." Sometimes an actor will freeze and immediately become immobilized by alternatives. When this happens, some suggested solutions include telling the actor, "If you breathe between the two words or take a beat, it will come out perfect," or suggesting an entirely different approach to the moment. It may not be visible, but it may just produce the required results. Giving an actor a "line reading" is frowned upon and is considered insulting by professional actors. On rare occasions, it may be the only practical solution to get to a result within a reasonable amount of time; and on other rare occasions, an actor may simply request an interpretation of the line by the director as an indication of how to proceed.

As a general rule, let the actors find their way without excessive instruction or rationalization by the director. It's the actor's job to understand the character and behave accordingly. If the actors are having a problem, take them through the moment and then let them go on. Looking to the director for help with every line or gesture is unprofessional and a waste of the company's time and money. If an actor has to be coddled this way, there better be a damned good reason.

Rather than use the term *amateur*, let's just say there are actors with little experience and not much exposure to the creative process. They lack seasoning and haven't learned the lessons, shortcuts, and tricks that professionals have acquired over years in their art. Nevertheless, because they have been cast in the production for whatever reason (looks, connections, good luck, or actual talent), they are now part of the unit and have to be smoothly integrated into the collaborative process.

As we have said above, there are several ways to accomplish this short of simply barking instructions such as "Just hit your marks," "Don't look into the camera," and "Don't step on the other actor's lines." It takes only a few moments to quietly explain to the novice why these things are important, as well as a host of other things. If the reason for doing something is not immediately apparent to the actor or the director, remember that acting is the world's second oldest profession, and every rule has a historic reason and tradition. Some of the rules listed below may seem arbitrary and external, and in truth, they may be. Regardless, they are part of both the common courtesies of the profession and the basic vocabulary of movement and gesture that every actor should know, if not follow. They are the foundation of behavior for actors.

- Never leave the set without informing or seeking permission from the appropriate stage manager or assistant director.

- Never start a cross on your downstage leg.*

- Do not attempt to work while in a state of consciousness altered by alcohol or drugs. You can kill your career, or other people. (Like all of these rules, there are notable and ignoble exceptions—by persons whose temperaments and psyche can "handle" drugs and drink—but most people can't, and shouldn't even try. A brief or ruinous career or an injured colleague is too high a price to pay for guessing wrong about your capabilities.)

- When looking at another actor in close-up, concentrate only on one eye (usually the eye closest to the camera).**

- Don't block or upstage yourself.

---

* A holdover from Victorian-era stagecraft, it makes the body appear more fluid in movement.

** When watching someone's face, one's natural tendency is to try and watch "the whole head." The result is an imperceptible back-and-forth flickering of the eyes, which appears distracting and nervous when magnified on a screen close-up. Nevertheless, you will see this shifting of eyes all the time in movies and television.

- Find your light.

- Know your lines.

- Don't look down for your marks.

- Never be late to a set, better to be early; and always check in with the makeup, hair, and wardrobe departments before heading for refreshment and immediately upon return to the set.

- Be available to be off-camera for close-ups of other actors in the scenes; this is simply common courtesy.

As for normal professional conduct onstage or on set, the director or producer should make sure that assistants and coordinators instruct the actors as to what is expected of them. Deviations and misbehaviors should be immediately noted and checked. Mistakes are tolerable; bad habits are not.

Most of the preceding is applicable at every level of experience. The *amateur* actor, by definition, is someone whose primary interest and vocation is elsewhere, and he or she will not consciously pursue the profession beyond the rare opportunity that occasionally comes along. The *novice* is someone whose intent is to enter the profession, but has not yet accumulated the experience and wisdom that distinguishes the *professional*. In fact, one of the most common (and hard to earn) compliments offered by technicians and crew to a new actor is "You're a pro."

In the appendices to this workbook, you will find several collections of standard behavioral guidelines for the profession, from both theater and films. If you are working with entry-level colleagues, a close study of "the rules" is a useful, even necessary, mutual exercise.

Both the amateur and the novice need to learn the vocabulary and basic behaviors of the profession. The novice's motivation is simple—he or she wants to learn because it's a chosen profession, even a calling. Amateurs are less motivated—they're not in the game for their lifetime. They find themselves on a stage or set for a variety of circumstances that may or may not be related to their acting talent: they "look the part," they may be famous in another field (sports figures and musical artists are the most common choices, for economic or marketing reasons), or they may be connected to someone with executive authority who thinks they'd "work" in the part.

Famous or celebrity amateurs require special attention. They've achieved recognition or popularity in their profession, they are accustomed to honors and attention, and their skills (as ballplayers, rock stars, or politicians) are obvious. Their skills as actors, directors, writers, or bosses may be less obvious or even nonexistent, but it's useful to show some respect and guide them to favorable results, without being condescending or arbitrary. Be aware that there's a thin line between explanation and condescension; even the average celebrity has a working knowledge of how cameras work and is used to performing in public. If there's something simple that he or she doesn't understand, it's best to explain it privately and not talk down to him or her in front of the rest of the company.

To the working director, it doesn't matter if the novice or amateur is the financier's nephew, Miss Universe, a champion golfer, or a local dentist who bears an unfortunate resemblance to the character cliché specified in the script. Every actor should be treated with a modicum of dignity and respect as a professional; this includes extras and background players. Note that in the US, union rules often require that extras and background players be addressed by assistant directors, and if a director gives specific business or direction to an extra, there are boring financial consequences involving additional pay.

In smaller or nonunion independent feature-length and short films, the lines between speaking and nonspeaking roles, and even crew, may blur or overlap. Production personnel may be utilized as extras, and actors may lend a hand with props and scenery; everyone's working on the same film. In every case, the boss is still the person calling the shots and making production decisions that affect the budget. In the small or independent production, he or she is not bound by studio-era rules about job categories, overtime, extras, meal penalties, and the like.

Managing Actors' Problems, Twenty-One Bad Habits

There is a broad spectrum of solutions available for most artistic problems. If you are lucky, the answer will be "Louder," "Softer," "Faster," "Slower," "More," or "Less." In the practical world, every problem is unique and requires its own solutions. For example, a young director working in television was faced with a guest star/leading lady whose success was based on a series of charming performances in feature films. This time she was in a television half-hour comedy in which the script and the jokes were highly structured. It was the star's practice to ad-lib, improvise, and tinker with her dialog during the coverage of her scenes.

"This," she explained, "is how I keep it fresh and interesting for myself."

Her experimentation with the dialog was destroying the careful cadence and sequence of lines upon which clever comedy depends. She would fumble a straight line or setup and change the structure of a punch line to the point where it was no longer funny. The young director despaired; how was he going to get through the day's work and get the jokes right?

An older, wiser staff writer on the set offered to speak to the actress about her dialog. During the next break, he took her aside with a copy of the script and they chatted quietly. On the next take, and for the rest of her days on the show, she was letter perfect in her lines, didn't change a word, and delivered every punch line perfectly.

"What did you say to her?" the young director asked the writer, who responded, "I love what you're doing with the dialog, it's really keeping it fresh, but when you say it that way, I think it makes you look, um, kind of heavy, not fat or plump, but it's taking you in that direction . . ."

The young director said, "You told her ad-libs make her look fat?"

The writer said, "Exactly. It's a sure way to keep actresses faithful to the dialog."

The director asked, "What about male actors, what do you tell them?"

The writer shrugged and said, "It's simple. I just tell them that their changes to the dialog make them look older."

Solutions to actors' problems tend to fall into two categories: modest (compassionate and gently suggestive) or aggressive (brusque and specific). Let's examine the Twenty-One Bad Habits that you'll encounter in some actors, all of which can be summed up as "a failure to look, listen, react, or respond." Here's the list:

1. Acting by making sounds instead of saying words on the breath.

2. Imitating your own best performance.

3. Imitating someone else's best performance.

4. Working at acting ("What I'm doing is so-o-o-o hard . . .").

5. Waiting to act (not listening).

6. Missing the marks.

7. Ignoring the technical.

8. Obsessing with the technical ("Are we on a 50-millimeter lens?")

9. Incurable ad-libbing.

10. Overacting.

11. Underacting (or simply failing to act, "walking through it," relying on persona or presence to carry the scene).

12. Failing to read and understand the entire text (not just one's own speeches).

13. Failing to prepare (not doing homework, making ignorant choices or no choice at all).

14. Letting go of character (dropping out of character when other actors are speaking).

15. Failing to be considerate of fellow actors (not being there for off-camera dialog if requested, eating garlic or a gorgonzola burger when the first shot after lunch is a kissing close-up).

16. Judging the character (assigning a broad stereotype or cliché to the character, such as a leering villain or a jut-jawed hero).

17. Failing to come to a consensus on the character's physicalization (quibbling over the character's wardrobe, hair, or makeup).

18. Playing with props; pointing or brandishing weapons; failing to understand how the prop works; being careless with weapons, pyrotechnics, and large, unwieldy objects.

19. Being self-obsessed.

20. Lacking situational awareness—not understanding the setting (poise, walk, and stance are different in a fine restaurant then they are in an automotive muffler shop. Prepare for the environment).

21. Failing to coordinate dialogue, activity, and action (also known as "walking and talking").

There is an issue that poses problems for some but not all actors and directors. Sexually suggestive or explicit performance is second nature to those working in the adult entertainment community (sometimes referred to as "porn"). To the rest of the entertainment community, the complexities of shooting nude scenes and intimate sex acts pose particular problems. There are performers whose personal religious or moral standards simply prohibit it and who will not, under any circumstances, waive their beliefs for the purposes of entertainment. Some will go so far as to prohibit the use of a stand-in or body double, arguing that the illusion of their personal appearance is the same as their actual persona. To avoid confrontation on these issues, it's best to come to a complete (and contractual) understanding of the requirements of the part before hiring the actor. SAG-AFTRA, the consolidated actors' union, has a specific nudity clause in the standard actors' contract that the actor must initial at the time of signing, confirming the understanding that the part requires explicit nudity or sexual exposure.

Keep in mind that actors will say anything to get a part; they will claim abilities they don't have (horseback riding, fencing, motorcycling, juggling, etc.), and agree to "tasteful" nudity or other exposure. When confronted on the set with a big horse, a pointed blade, a Harley-Davidson, or a set of bowling pins, the truth comes out, and valuable shooting time is wasted or lost when trying to remedy a situation that should never have been permitted to occur.

In big-budget productions, there is time and money for specialized coaching, or lessons, or the use of exact physical body doubles. In other situations, this can be a huge drain on patience and resources, and have important (and negative) consequences on the actual scene(s) to be shot. Rather than try and work around an awkward or impossible situation, it's always preferable to confirm abilities and intentions by testing before hiring. As for nudity, it should be specified both in the script and in the contract, understood by all the parties, and confirmed by test shots or a swimsuit audition for both male and female actors. No director should have to bully or deceive an actor into appearing nude or in a sexually explicit scene; no actor should accept a role without completely understanding the ramifications and requirements of the text.

It's always a good idea to close a set or restrict the personnel when shooting sensitive material, unless the actor(s) completely accepts the exposure to a full crew. (Sally Kellerman's exposure in the film version of M*A*S*H was staged and shot in front of the full crew and the entire ensemble cast—which included this male author. It was understood it would be one take, and Ms. Kellerman used her embarrassment and discomfort to energize her performance, carrying it forward into her next scene in the HQ tent where she offers to resign her commission. It remains a memorable scene in a memorable motion picture.)

Whenever there is nudity, unless specified otherwise, there should be strict prohibitions or control of still photographs, cellphone and video cameras, and on-set documentary filming (tabloid TV, "making of. . . ," etc.), unless the entire cast is openly amenable and agrees unanimously to coverage. This agreement should be in writing as a paragraph in the employment contract or a separate release form.

The following table lists the "bad habits" and suggests two approaches for how to handle them: a compassionate or caring remark, or a more biting, direct statement. While these will work verbatim, readers are encouraged to study the tone and character of the comments and come up with their own variants. Note to actors who are studying this: you're not getting any secret insights, just some advance notice as to some things you may be doing unconsciously and what you may expect to hear. If you say these things to yourself, you'll be one step ahead of your omnipotent collaborator, your acting boss, or the director.

The Bad Habit	The Sensitive Approach	The Aggressive Solution	The Reason Why
1. Acting by making sounds (using sigh, breaths, moans, groans, and similar effects in place of or as punctuation to the text).	"Use your breath to say the words, not to make the sounds before the words."	"Just say the lines as written, without embellishment."	The actor tends to lose momentum when adding breaths or sounds and has to reinvent or reestablish the pace of the speech all over again.
2. Imitating your own best performance.	"You've been successful with that approach before, but it may not be appropriate for this scene now."	"Very good, but not what we're looking for here."	It was appropriate, or even brilliant, at a different time in the script or in another production, but this is a new moment.

The Bad Habit	The Sensitive Approach	The Aggressive Solution	The Reason Why
3. Imitating someone else's best performance.	"That's not you."	"It's not you, it's not right for the character, find something else to do."	Actors who are copying another actor's performance are being impressionists and not doing original work in interpreting the character.
4. Working at acting ("What I'm doing is so-o-o-o hard…")	"You're letting the process show; you're showing us technique, not the emotions or what your character is feeling."	"You're upstaging yourself. Bring it down. Do less, thank you."	Less is more, and an overelaborate or strenuous presentation takes away from the moment and makes the audience disengage.
5. Waiting to act (not listening).	"I need you to listen more carefully to the other actor(s) and be more present in the scene."	"Don't just act while you're talking. Look, listen, and respond all the time you're in the scene."	The reaction shot is an important component of editing dialog. An actor who fails to completely commit to the scene forces the editor to ignore his or her footage, and winds up cut out of the scene. Conversely, an actor who's always "present" can always be used in a cutaway or for a reaction shot.

The Bad Habit	The Sensitive Approach	The Aggressive Solution	The Reason Why
6. Missing marks.	"You should sense where you should be, trust yourself to find the right spot . . . remember the rehearsal, and get a sense of where the camera and the other actors are."	"You're not in the light, you're not in the scene. You're blocking the shot. Somebody show him [her]."	The camera requires certain placement actors, lights, and related paraphernalia; this may also involve the movement of the camera and the staging of other actors and background. There's a lot of composition even in the most basic frame; it can get very complicated if an actor is out of place.
7. Ignoring the technical.	"I need you to be aware of the many elements in the scene besides your dialog: there are props, lights, other actors, camera moves, and scenery; take a moment and rehearse with these things until you're comfortable."	"If you can only do one thing at a time, tell me and I'll restage the scene."	The actor is only one element of a scene; the work of the other artists and technicians has to be accommodated to complete the director's vision and the writer's script.

The Bad Habit	The Sensitive Approach	The Aggressive Solution	The Reason Why
8. Obsessing with the technical ("Are we on a 50-millimeter lens?")	"Please concentrate on your dialogue and relationship with the other actor(s); we're all professionals here, and everyone else will take care of their job if you take care of yours."	"It's none of your business. Just say the lines."	It's a distraction to the actor if he or she is worrying about all the production elements rather than focusing on his or her performance.
9. Incurable ad-libbing.	"Thanks for adding that last bit, but I think we'll just stick to the author's text for this scene."	"Where does it say that? I don't see it in the script. Don't say it again."	The production script is the result of a great deal of creative effort, and the producer expects to see it shot as written. Last-minute elaborations on the text are neither useful nor insightful. *However:* the occasional in-character ad-lib by a clever actor caught up in the moment may add a joke or insight to the scene, so while the practice should be discouraged, the director should be open to the moment.

The Bad Habit	The Sensitive Approach	The Aggressive Solution	The Reason Why
10. Overacting.	"Could you bring it down a notch and do a little less, please."	"When I want Gloria Swanson in Sunset Boulevard, I'll tell you."	An overaggressive performance by an actor takes the audience out of the moment and calls attention to itself, rather than contributing to the whole.
11. Underacting (or simply failing to act, "walking through it," relying on persona or presence to carry the scene).	"Would you try it again and concentrate more on the objective, and its importance to the story."	"You're walking through it. Let's try acting; make some choices, any choices. Thank you."	An underwhelming performance damages a production as much as an overstated performance, and for the same reason: it takes the audience out of the moment and fails to engage the viewer.
12. Failing to read and understand the entire text (not just one's own speeches).	"You should be integrating your action into that of the others in the story, and be aware of the significance of what you're doing in this scene. Remember where we are in the story."	"Do you know what we're doing here? If you don't know, ask someone who knows."	Most films are shot out of sequence, so there's no clear line from one day's work to the next. For a coherent narrative, each section or scene has to be appropriate to its place in the story, not the shooting schedule. Usually, the primary responsibility for tracking the story falls on the director, who must be able to enlighten members of the cast or crew who are uncertain.

The Bad Habit	The Sensitive Approach	The Aggressive Solution	The Reason Why
13. Failing to prepare (not doing home-work, making inappropriate choices or no choice at all).	"Take a moment and let's rehearse this again before we shoot it."	"Pay attention! Get it right this time."	An underachieving member of the team drags the entire effort down, so every effort should be made to engage the actor and make him or her work at or above his or her best level of competence.
14. Letting go of character (dropping out of character when other actors are speaking).	"We're all in this together; stay in the scene; keep your energy up."	"Excuse me; do you know where you are? Pay attention!"	If an actor drops character or is not "in the scene," it makes it almost impossible to cut to a useful close-up or reaction, and it also saps the energy of the ensemble.
15. Failing to be considerate of fellow actors (not being there for off-camera dialog if requested, eating garlic or a gorgonzola burger when the first shot after lunch is a kissing close-up).	"Let's think about each other, shall we? Is everyone comfortable, or is there something someone might be doing differently? See me privately, please."	"What are you thinking? Take care of that before the next take."	It's the director's responsibility to make sure every element of the production is functioning at optimal level. If there's dissatisfaction between actors or crew, the reason has to be found and the dysfunction cured. If you don't know why some-one's unhappy about something, ask. Find out. Fix it.

The Bad Habit	The Sensitive Approach	The Aggressive Solution	The Reason Why
16. Judging the character (assigning a broad stereotype or cliché to the character, such as a leering villain or a jut-jawed hero).	"That's a rather obvious approach; let's try and work on something a little more interesting, something we haven't seen before, okay?"	"When I want Gloria Swanson in *Sunset Boulevard*, I'll tell you." (No disrespect to Ms. Swanson. It's to her credit that her char-acterization, not her actual performance, is memorably extreme.)	It helps the work if it's completely original, which rules out obvious choices and snap judgments by actors; the occasional cliché, like the occasional ad-lib, might be helpful to the overall production, but as a general rule, avoid the obvious.
17. Failing to come to a consensus on the character's physicalization (quibbling over the character's wardrobe, hair, or makeup).	"I think you're letting your personal preferences overrule the logical choices the team has agreed on for the character.	"No. That's not right. Stop that. What happened to the hat we got for you?"	A unified approach is necessary if the story is properly served. There's no room for egocentric or thoughtless choices that disrupt the unity of the production.

The Bad Habit	The Sensitive Approach	The Aggressive Solution	The Reason Why
18. Playing with props; pointing or brandishing weapons; failing to understand how the prop works; being careless with weapons, pyrotechnics, and large unwieldy objects.	"You okay with that thing? Show us what you're going to do with it. Let's have the expert here show you how it works (prop master, armorer, pyro-technician)."	"Don't touch that! Rehearse with that guy and don't do anything unless he says it's okay. Tell me what I just said. Thank you."	Weapons, explosives, and complicated machinery can maim or kill; union movies have strict requirements for handling firearms; indie and short films are less restrictive, but they can be more dangerous if qualified armorers and technicians aren't in the budget.
19. Being self-obsessed.	"I wish we could all share your outlook and approach, but perhaps it requires some moderation."	"Who the hell do you think you are?"	A star vehicle is not about just one person. Even a one-character monologue requires a collaborative team to realize the final effect.
20. Lacking situational awareness (not being aware of the setting: one behaves differently in a fine restaurant than in a coal mine).	"Is what you're doing really appropriate here? Let's think of another way to react to the other actors, the location, or the situation."	"Where the hell do you think we are?"	The story is best served if everyone's involved in the same vision or the textual concept. In the end, everyone (including the director) is serving the script and the production, and agreement is essential.

The Bad Habit	The Sensitive Approach	The Aggressive Solution	The Reason Why
21. Failing to coordinate dialogue, activity, and action (also known as "walking and talking").	"Let's rehearse the action and activity with all the props; don't take a bite until we're shooting—make sure it's edible, and not a prop that's been shellacked or varnished or sprayed."	"Let me see you do that before we shoot it. Is that food? Don't touch it!"	The seemingly normal activities of life are not easily replicated in a tight performance situation and require rehearsal; some actors have no trouble coordinating, others require special attention, and some can't walk and chew gum at the same time.

CHAPTER 11

Managing Extras:
The Madness of Crowds

In the epic film *Dr. Zhivago*, David Lean created a large-scale ensemble crowd scene in the railroad coaches of a train bound for Siberia. As the camera moves through the cars, a panorama of the Russian population is revealed. People from every strata of society are seen—peasants, soldiers, the middle class, children, beggars, and the nobility—all with vivid clarity. This is not just great photography; the humanity, background, and experience of every person in the frame is apparent. Some mutter, some pray, some cry, some stare with blank eyes, while others fight. Every background player has a moment in which he or she is revealed as a person and not a symbol.

Lean achieved this effect, we are told, by spending an enormous amount of time watching local Russian theater productions and selecting actors whose physicality matched his vision. Without speaking any Russian, and working through interpreters, Lean selected dozens of individuals and assigned each one of them a personal history—a character that he or she would play in the train.

Even though the ensemble was comprised of actors, the reality of the visual effect is impressive for its truthfulness and complexity. Directors should remember that every person in a crowd scene is an individual, with a backstory and a history that brings him or her to that place at that time. By discussing each individual's background, the director "opens up" the crowd into what is its true nature: a mass of individuals forced by time and circumstance into the scene.

Modern filmmaking and SAG-AFTRA rules limit a director's ability to be as thorough as David Lean was. CGI and visual effects can create crowds. Modern scripts in which the principal characters move through and interact with a crowd or mob are very few. Epics like Zhivago may never be made again, or be made rarely, and then only as large-budget studio productions. Nevertheless, the lesson to the director is clear. Know everything about everybody in the frame.

The resources once available to Lean, Cecil B. DeMille, Akira Kurosawa, and Sergei Bondarchuk are unlikely to be made available to contemporary filmmakers again. In the past, when many companies shot epic spectacles in Italy, the Italians developed a system of dividing crowds of extras into small teams or squads, each with a captain. It made directing crowd scenes simple: the director would talk to the captains, the captains would talk to their teams, and in this way, a thousand extras could be easily organized. If you think about it, it's a direct lineal descendant of the organization of a Roman legion, and if the

Roman legions conquered an empire, their organizational style can certainly be used by filmmakers in their own territorial expansion. When a modern director is faced with a crowd scene, the first question is, "How much of this can be accomplished with visual effects and CGI." Once that has been settled, the remaining task is how to manage a crowd of extras to create a realistic illusion of a mob, regiment, or tribe. Here are some tips:

- **Delegate Authority:** Give the assistants and ADs the knowledge of what you want, and trust them to communicate it down through the chain of command. A screen mob is like an army; it needs orders on how, where, and when to charge.

- **Avoid Wide Shots:** Your every impulse will be to go up on the crane or wide on the stairway, like Eisenstein on the Odessa steps in *Battleship Potemkin*. There is nothing sadder or lonelier than a clump of extras trying to look like a crowd and failing to fill the frame. A few hundred people in an open exterior look like stragglers, not an army. It is depressing to consider how many human bodies it takes to fill a town square, a street (even on the back lot), a stadium, an auditorium, or Times Square. We have all seen that moment in a low budget or television production when the pep rally, angry mob, or stadium crowd is shown with a sea of empty space behind it, or twenty uniformed extras pretend to be a regiment.

- **Stay Low:** A viewpoint that moves through the crowd can hint at the size and number of people without actually showing them. Foreground figures, violent action, and rapid movement—all contribute to a sense of "the mob."

- **Use Sound:** Combined with low-angle and eye-level camera views, the effective use of crowd sounds (battle cries, cheers, and thundering feet or hooves) can contribute to the convincing illusion of a mob. Bottom line? Sound effects are cheaper than extras.

- **Attention to Detail:** On-camera crowd scenes can be brought to life by staging vignettes within the larger action. Think of the large battle scenes in "sword and sandal" epics where the big action is intercut with individual soldiers struggling to the death or a single chariot plunging through the melee. Note that this violent action is nothing compared to the real-world off-camera reaction when there aren't enough toilets, box lunches, or vans to serve your crowd.

- **Keep Your Word:** If you are shooting a large crowd of extras from an agreed-upon angle, don't suddenly decide you want the camera looking the other way. There is too much planning involved to arbitrarily change the coverage. Don't promise a wrap time; crowd scenes are notoriously unpredictable and can stretch for days. Since most extras tend to be undisciplined or inexperienced actors, they will simply walk away from disorganized jobs for which they are underpaid and mistreated. Keep your extras and crew warm, fed, and respected. Then, like Henry the Fifth, you can cry, "Once more into the breach," with the expectation that you will be followed, not shot in the back.

- **Keep Everyone Safe:** A large crowd scene is, by definition, dramatic and exciting, or of great significance. It usually requires multiple camera coverage, camera platforms, and stage props and equipment, even livestock. When you think "crowd scene," you are probably talking about a battle, a mob, a riot, a convention, or a revolution—or some or all of these. There is danger when large crowds of people move anywhere. Make sure all contingencies are provided for, and try to budget enough time for stop-and-go rehearsal, at half speed, before committing to full-out action. Tell your AD and cast, "Let's just walk through this so we all know what we are doing" (your camera crews will also thank you for the opportunity to preview the action). It is usually not practical to do retakes of the Normandy Invasion in *Saving Private Ryan* or the Burning of Atlanta in *Gone With the Wind*—and that's just people. Cattle stampedes and herds of wild animals are best shot in one take with multiple cameras. Try telling two thousand angry water buffalo, "Back to your starting marks, please."

- **Planning, Planning, Planning (No Surprises, Please):** Crowd scenes, more than any other sequences you will be shooting, require careful planning, the advice of experts, proper permits, and much longer to-do lists for the production department. Whether you are a student filmmaker, wrangling twelve people for a party scene for which they'll be paid in beer; or the director of a major studio version of *The Gulf War*, plan the sequence more carefully than anything else you will be shooting. It should never come as a surprise when you urgently need medics, port-a-potties, a means of evacuation for the injured, or a place for the Seventh Calvary to get out of the sun. When that time comes, it's too late to improvise. Have the details covered. Pray that you'll never need to airlift an injured stunt man or an elderly extra with a heart attack to a trauma center. Know that if these misfortunes occur, they can be managed efficiently. Sharing information is crucial—it's tempting to keep the extras ignorant of some major element of the scene (so you can get an "honest reaction" to an unforeseen event), but when the ship sinks, the pyrotechnics explode, and the wild horses stampede, it's criminally unfair to traumatize the crowd in the name of realism.

Finally, for dedicated students of filmmaking, you are urged to view *The Battle of Algiers*, an Italian film directed by Gillo Pontecorvo and written by Pontecorvo and Franco Solinas in 1966. It's a historical action dramatization of the conflict between French colonial interests and the citizens of Algiers, which resulted in the termination of a centuries-old colonization of North Africa by the French. Because of the big, populous scenes of riots and battles, much of the action appears to be taken from period newsreel footage—except that Pontecorvo includes a proud statement in the credits: *none* of the footage is documentary! However spontaneous and lifelike it seemed, it was all staged by the director, with extras and actors, and using a camera style that made it seem immediate, unrehearsed, and (most importantly) *real*. The illusion is near-perfect.

CHAPTER 12

Improvisation
as a Tool

Sooner or later, the suggestion will come from somewhere, or
you will think of it yourself: "Why don't we improvise?" This is
evident in a slew of recent works from Judd Apatow and a twenty-
first-century generation of writers, performers, and directors
whose roots are in improvisational comedy—from companies
such as Second City, The Groundlings, Upright Citizen's Brigade,
and others who owe their inspiration to Christopher Guest and
Spinal Tap. Then there are the works of Robert Altman, John
Cassavetes, and British filmmaker Mike Leigh, who's been nom-
inated four times for an Academy Award for original screenplay
writing, on films that were the product of a long collaborative
period of improvisation with a repertory company of actors.

It is no accident that great playwrights have historically
worked with a company or repertory group of actors. A partial
list that should convince the skeptic that a company of actors can
be a playwright's most useful asset includes William Shakespeare,

Moliere, and Eugene O'Neill, and modern contemporaries such as David Mamet, Sam Shepherd, Mel Brooks, and the Coen Brothers. In Hollywood's Golden Era, think John Ford (the John Wayne Western cycle), Elia Kazan's black-and-white films with Brando and Actor's Studio members, Orson Welles's Mercury Theatre ensemble, and John Sturges's elevation of character actors to stars in *The Magnificent Seven* and *The Great Escape*.

There are two major rivers of improvisation, flowing from two major sources. One is the headwaters of the Stanislavsky System, Lee Strasburg and the Actor's Studio "Method," and the Sanford Meisner Technique. The other is the great mainstream that sprang from the well dug by Viola Spolin in her seminal book *Improvisation for the Theater*, which was perfected by her son, director Paul Sills, in his work with the original companies of The Second City in Chicago and his own "Story Theater" productions. In addition, much is owed to David Shephard's work with the Compass Theater in Chicago and St. Louis, with fellow actors and directors Elaine May and Ted Flicker and their "Kitchen Rules." Those streams eventually became the basis for a school of comic and serious acting that many (including the authors) believe has replaced the Method as the defining acting style of the present day.

Stanislavskian improvisation was originally intended as a technique for actors to discover, embellish, and refine their characters. As such, it has a tendency to encourage overreaching, "ranting," and a host of actors' indulgences that are useful for character development but of less help to the entire work, the ensemble, or the writer's text. If anything, this type of "inside-out" improvisation usually turns into an exercise for adding endless dialogue, as the actors rhapsodize about their backstories/histories, motivations, feelings, emotions, and reactions.

On the other hand, Spolin-based theatrical improvisation has evolved into a generally comedic technique that has as many, if not more, offshoots and descendants than Stanislavsky's Method. One can point to The Second City, The Premise, The Committee, Improv Olympics, Upright Citizens Brigade, and the players who went on to fill the ranks of writers, producers, and directors of almost every situation comedy and late-night talk show on network and cable television for the last thirty years, as well as many of the highest-profile comedians working in films and television over the same period.

All that said, it should be understood that for the purposes of this workbook, it is Spolin's, Compass Theater's, and Second City's theatrical improvisation rules that provide the most useful director/actor interface. Like all "rules," they're subject to change and modification over time, but for the last half-century, they've proved their value.

1. Never deny or negate the reality established onstage.

2. Think or say "Yes, and . . . ," and add information or make an active choice.

3. Don't "write" the scene; your partner can't know what's in your head; deal only with the momentary reality onstage (be "in the now").

4. Know *who* you are.

5. Know *where you are.*

6. Know what you're doing (based on what has been presented in the improvisation, suggested by the audience or the director, or agreed upon between the players).

7. Don't sacrifice the troupe's cohesion by indulging your ego to score a laugh or make a point; it's a group effort, always.

8. Never abandon your partner. There may occasionally be a good reason to make an exit and leave one person alone onstage, but generally, it's a bad idea. Like the elite military, always bring back your dead and wounded; don't flee the field and leave an actor to "die" in the theatrical sense. Take your partner with you.

Be true to the text or the script and don't "change the words," but as an exercise, work in the silences between the words: look, listen, and respond to the words. The actor shouldn't be seen as "acting"; he or she should be seen as if the moment is just happening, the way it does in life. It is these luminescent close-ups of a great actor's face in attentive repose, simply being totally present and in the moment, that create a memorable performance. It's not just the eloquent recitation of lines of text.

For reference, here are a few reasons to encourage actors to improvise:

- To help them memorize the lines. Example: You might have them improvise the character with the other actor(s), then improvise the scene, then return to the text as written.

- To add to the scene (help the actors) by giving them tools. Example: You might give them a "secret" about the character ("You have an incurable disease"), an outside motivation ("You're being followed"), something about the other character ("You're lovers who just broke up"), or the like. It's not necessary for this to be something that's present in the script.

- Additional exercises:
  1. The actor prepares a shopping or to-do list for the character.
  2. The actors play the scene in pantomime (to isolate the specific necessary elements).
  3. Actors substitute gibberish syllables ("blah-blah-blah" is a good choice) for the text. The actors are instructed to convey every subtle meaning in the text using sounds, not speech; in so doing, they isolate the gist of the scene and the underlying nature of their lines and responses.

Technically, it's useful if the cameraman and department heads are present for the late stages of the improvisational work. They may be stimulated to think less literally about the scene, and it will be helpful to get additional input into how the actors' insights and solutions add dimension to the scene(s).

The proliferation of new digital cameras and their ability to record in available light multiplies the possibilities for improvisational moments or even entire scenes to be integrated into the production without elaborate rehearsal, possibly without rehearsal at all. If the entire company is made aware of the sets or locations and understands their potentials and limitations, a whole film can be "improvised" with only a simple outline, character notes, and an agreed-upon theme. In a strange and wonderful way, the innovations of the twenty-first century may help the art of film return to its anarchic roots, when Charlie Chaplin could take his crew to a real event (a soapbox derby, in one notable example) and insert actors into the proceedings, shooting unobtrusively and producing a story with a sprawling backdrop to enhance its basic comic charm.

If the legal hurdles and insurance and union complications of modern mass media can be resolved, there's no telling what astonishing works lie ahead. If we were to venture a prediction, comedies will lead the way; then small, personal dramas; and then (possibly) action epics that use real environments. As if to support the contention that "everything's been done before," writer-director Haskell Wexler made a film in 1969 titled *Medium Cool*. A long-time activist and passionate supporter of civil rights and social justice, Wexler's semiautobiographical story is about a cameraman whose personal life becomes entwined with the assignment he's covering, the 1968 National Democratic Convention held in Chicago.

Unlike Gillo Pontecorvo, who "re-created" reality, Wexler and his cast and crew went on location, shooting park exteriors during the 1968 civil riots and unrest that accompanied the convention. This wasn't second-unit background footage; this was first-unit stuff, with principal actors and the director colliding and interacting with citizens, the Chicago police, and all the forces of law and order that caused a historic television experience for the whole nation, watching live on network television. A close listening to the soundtrack will reveal the warning shouted to the director by his crew: in the production audio track, as tear-gas shells explode, you can hear the words "Haskell, it's real!..." mixed in with the shouts and screams from the crowd.

It's probable we'll be seeing more like this: stories from all sides of the political spectrum acted against the real backdrop of civil unrest, war, revolution, and natural catastrophes. In an oddly intriguing way, stories will be created in which "acts of God" will dictate much of the action, rather than screenwriters and producers. As in every good improvisation, the reality of the moment will direct the actors' lines and action, and the best boss will be the one who can organize members of the company to immerse themselves in events, recognize the best "moments" as they occur, and then get everyone out of the action safe and uninjured to review the footage and make it into a coherent whole. That this is challenging is an understatement; we can't wait to see it happen.

CHAPTER 13

Documentaries

Meanwhile, whether creating a reality or using an existing reality for a fictional narrative, the documentary (or nonfiction) film is an appealing form for any boss. It apparently has no actors to cast, no script to follow, and an informal structure that will develop on the fly. All one has to do is start shooting and the story will tell itself. All of these assertions are mistaken. The documentary is like any other conscious construct; it's telling a story. The story is theoretically based in reality, and the pretense is that the filmmaker is simply recording "the truth" as it happens.

The defining characteristic of the documentary film is the assertion that the real world is being recorded with minimal intervention by the filmmaker; the truth is that like any story, a documentary has an inherent premise, a cast of characters, and a narrative form. It is not enough to "just start shooting." The documentarian makes choices of what and when to shoot, which people will tell their story, and what message is to be taken away by the audience. In some forms of documentary, a place or an event or a situation will be the starting point, and the narrative will evolve during the shooting and editing. The editorial choices of the filmmaker are much more involved and complicated then in a traditional fictional narrative movie. Unforeseen events may take place, the dialog spoken by characters in the film is unscripted, and the audience may be led to conclusions and the footage may lead to a narrative point that was never apparent at the onset.

A filmmaker and photographer named Barry Feinstein, who shot the Bob Dylan documentary *Eat the Document*, made this point: "I'd like the camera crew to wear black jumpsuits, like a SWAT team, with the words 'Cinema Verité' on the back and 'Look Away, I'm Invisible' on the chest." It was his way of defining a style of documentary filmmaking called cinema verité, which is one of the principal forms of the genre.

The other documentary forms include narrated presentation and direct observation without narration. In all forms of documentaries, individuals may speak to an off-camera interrogator or to a visible filmmaker. Sometimes the audio track of the speaker off-camera is edited out, so only the person speaking on screen is heard, without a disembodied voice asking a question or prompting a response.

Dialog may be recreated by an actor reading text the character has written (e.g., the letters of Union and Confederate troops, read over the visuals in the Ken Burns series *The Civil War*). It should be noted that the very title of Mr. Burns's documentary makes a political statement; the conflict he describes in twelve hours of brilliant documentary filmmaking is called "The War Between the States" or "The War of Northern Aggression" by Southerners, which illustrates the axiom "History is written by the winners." For an illustration of a contrarian documentary viewpoint, the German filmmaker Leni Rifenstahl made a powerful film titled *Triumph of the Will*, which was ostensibly about the 1938 Olympics but is filled with subliminal messages about the power and glory of Hitler and the Nazi State, and is studied for its technique to this day.

Ms. Rifenstahl's documentaries stand as powerful examples of how factual film can be manipulated to create an overwhelming narrative.

Often a documentary may be created from found footage and manipulated still photos, without any new material being shot. In these cases, the filmmaker supplies a spoken or musical accompaniment, which tells the story or supplements the visuals with additional information and musical scoring for emotional involvement. For example: a sequence of archival footage of the bombing of Pearl Harbor can position the film as an indictment of aggression by the Imperial Forces, or with a different sound track and narration can be a description of a triumphant victory by gallant Japanese airmen.

With the advent of new digital cameras and recording equipment, the documentarian can be ever more unobtrusive. Using hidden cameras, the filmmaker can be actually invisible to the subjects of the documentary; it is in this way that investigative journalists have made powerful statements about malpractice in commercial food processing plants, caught congressmen taking bribes, and observed drug deals and other criminal enterprises as they are happening.

The "invisible observer" or "cinema verité" style once mocked by Mr. Feinstein has evolved into an entire genre on television. The eavesdropping, surveillance-video style of documentary is compelling because it appeals to the voyeur in all of us. YouTube thrives on exactly this sort of keyhole-peeping footage.

The more conventional approach to a documentary is to find subject matter of interest and then explore it visually. This may involve archival footage combined with new material, interviews or quotes from participants, and perhaps a narrative summary and conclusion provided by the filmmaker.

The basic story elements that appeal to all audiences are character, place, and relationship.

A successful documentary, or any scene or story, combines these three elements in equal balance. It is also possible to be successful when one or two of the elements are so unique and intriguing that they carry the story. For example: an extremely vivid or engaging character (a hundred-year-old cowboy, a major political figure or movie star) may be all you need to tell the story. Similarly, an interesting place such as a submarine, a rain-forest research station, or a Chinese surfboard factory may be of sufficient interest to carry the narrative. And finally, when it comes to relationships, a blind person and his or her companion animal, a family intervention, or a platoon leader and his soldiers embody the kinds of intense and personal relationships that make for compelling viewing.

Like all films, documentaries are made within limits: there's a budget, a time schedule, research, and postproduction. In a documentary, the heaviest lifting is often in the research and editorial aspects, because it is often only after the fact, when the footage is reviewed, that a complete narrative suggests itself. A simple documentary that begins as a tutorial about mountain-climbing technique may turn into a biographical character sketch of an intrepid climber who invents new hardware to accomplish his goal.

An enjoyable example of this morphing process is a film that began as a documentary about the aspirations of a Jamaican bobsledding team; it turned into a delightful character study of the men who actually went to the winter Olympics representing an island on which it never snows: *Cool Runnings* (1996).

Sometimes, a filmmaker's documentary may become the inspiration for a larger-scale feature film, set in that world with those characters. In the United States, the civil rights movement inspired a number of feature films that had their roots in the work of documentarians who were recording the struggle.

Some things to remember when making a documentary:

- Determine early on if you are going to be a voyeur or a physical presence in the piece.

- Although you will be tempted to manipulate the reality, a true documentary filmmaker will not overly influence the characters or events that he or she is filming. There is one exception to this rule: when making a polemic or a political or opinion piece for the purposes of information or propaganda, with a selective point of view that limits material that might blur or diffuse the issue. This is a slippery slope; PETA, Michael Moore, Andrew Breitbart, Leni Rifenstahl, and the Swift Boat Veterans have all attracted anger and hostility because of their work. This is one area where the filmmakers' opinion and point of view really matters. Let your conscience (or lack of it) be your guide.

- Preparations for a documentary should include an outline that sets out a narrative thread, and lists the minimum audio and visual material required. With that list in hand, the filmmaker can decide what can be obtained from library or archival sources, and what new material must be shot.

- Don't talk down to the audience. It's unnecessary to have a narration tell us what is evident on the screen; audiences are smarter than you think.

- Avoid the temptation of leaving all the narrative work to a voiceover or printed onscreen information. If the truth is not evident in the footage, no amount of repetition and re-statement will convince the viewer otherwise. To a pacifist, footage of bleeding, wounded soldiers and civilians will overwhelm and deny any stirring declarations about the virtues of combat and the glories of war.

Let There Be Light, John Huston's masterful post–World War II documentary about combat soldiers hospitalized with neuro-psychiatric damage, was suppressed for decades—not because of its filmmaking, but because its content was disturbing. It showed that the results of combat may be profoundly disabling to some soldiers, even those without lasting physical injuries. It was what a later documentarian, Al Gore, called his work on global climate change: "an inconvenient truth."

- When interviewing people, make them comfortable and at ease. If it is a confrontational interview, be assured that whatever their pose or stance may be, it will eventually become secondary to their real message, as they become involved in what they have to say.

- If you can't hide the camera, hide your intentions—you want to minimalize your presence and your influence over what is happening.

- Never underestimate the value of accurately logging and recording all of your material. Quoting Joni Mitchell, "You don't know what you've got till it's gone."

- Be aware that there are laws that govern people's right of privacy, the use of trademarks, and copyright-protected material. Be sure that you obtain legal counsel and are aware of the forms, permissions, and releases that you must have if you are ever to publicly exhibit your work. Many films carry a form of insurance that compensates the producer for "errors and omissions." In budget shorthand, this is called E&O insurance. Don't film without it.

- The fact that you are filming "the real world" doesn't excuse you from protecting yourself against intrusion and interference. Try to control your filming environment—you don't want to lose a valuable, irreplaceable, or spontaneous moment because someone walks in front of the lens, there's unexpected noise, or an official intervenes in the production while it's in process.

• Some loss of control is inevitable when you are filming clandestinely or because obtaining the necessary permits and permission would jeopardize the integrity of your work or destroy the opportunity to film. Insurance won't protect you from criminal or civil suit for wrongdoing, although it may cover some of the cost of your defense (with a very high deductible!) It's also possible that the publicity that results from your being sued or jailed will help your film commercially. Distributors, financing sources, and exhibitors may become aware of your project without your spending a dime on marketing and promotion. The most immediate examples of this are documentaries that recorded a clandestine adventure (such as jumping off a bridge with a parachute or climbing a skyscraper unassisted) in which the participants broke the law and went ahead without permits or permissions (or insurance, probably) and filmed the results.

• Actions have consequences; plan for the eventualities. If you are going to jail or being ejected or physically beaten, protect the film[*] first, then the camera, then yourself. Note

---

[*] *Film* is a term of art in a changing technology; here it refers to whichever medium was used to record the sound and images: film, tape, chip, flash memory, cell phone, camcorder, and so forth.

that a second or third hidden camera in a discreet location will provide interesting footage, as well as a possible defense in civil or criminal prosecution later.

- Every living person seen onscreen must sign a release giving you permission to use his or her name or likeness. Ignore this requirement at your peril. It will fatally jeopardize the sale or any commercial exhibition of your film if you don't have releases from everyone, especially those persons depicted in an unflattering or accusatory way. Many filmmakers use an attractive or charming crew person to cajole the subject into signing the release. Don't go into the field without a stack of blank releases or forms. Even persons seen to be committing some sort of offense on camera, placed under arrest, and on their way to jail have signed personal release forms for televised police reality shows (*Cops*, for example). Chances are they have been offered something: the show's crew promises to inform relatives, donate bail money, or assist with obtaining counsel as an incentive to get that all-important signature. The people who don't sign releases? They're the ones with their faces optically blurred and voices altered or bleeped so as to be unrecognizable.

CHAPTER 14

Reality Programming: Neither Fish nor Fowl

In the last few decades, a form of television entertainment labeled "reality programming" has occupied huge blocks of prime-time broadcasting. Originally it began with a documentary-style recording of real people in real situations. The ancestor of all of these shows dates back to radio, a show called *Candid Microphone*.

The creator of the show, Allen Funt, made a successful transition to television using a hidden camera to record ordinary people's reactions to improbable setups. (The most memorable example was a "talking mailbox" that addressed passersby.) In time, *Candid Camera* was joined by similar shows, such as Dick Clark's *Bloopers and Practical Jokes*; the form survives on such shows as *Pranked*, which follows Allen Funt's sixty-year-old formula almost exactly.

Other reality formats include "reenactment" shows such as *Unsolved Mysteries*, *American Greed*, and *Divorce Court*, in which the episodes, based on true events, use actors to portray real people and re-create events that were never recorded in actuality.

The inherent theatricality of courtroom drama has been exploited in shows like *Judge Judy*, who kicked off a rash of imitators in black robes making decisions for people who would normally be clogging the calendars of small claims courts all across America. The plaintiffs and defendants are "real people," who've opted to have their cases decided by a TV judge on camera, and signed a waiver binding them to the unofficial verdict. Win or lose, they're usually paid a nominal fee for consenting to appear and allowing their legal issue(s) to be resolved by a television personality who may or not have real-world experience as a judge.

The ancient vaudeville tradition of "talent night" is a form that is more than a century old. It gave us similar radio and television shows—from *The Original Amateur Hour* and *A Night at The Apollo*, to *American Idol*, *America's Got Talent*, and many similar variants. All of these shows are variations on a central premise: the audience selects its favorite performers from a program of singers, dancers, and novelty acts, all of which are the basic ingredients of variety entertainment today. Advances in technology allow voting by phone and on the Internet, as well as the time-honored tradition of a master of ceremonies who asks the audience to judge "by your applause."

Another form of reality show is the faux-documentary examination of troubled souls: *Sober House*, *Intervention*, *Hoarders*, and similar programs come to mind.

There are also shows about competition. Originally, these were the simplistic beauty pageants—like *Miss America*, which later morphed into dozens of similar formats, from *Miss Universe* to versions for children and teenagers as well as ethnic groups. The "pageant" shows always included a competitive talent element, from baton twirling to interpretive dance.

The competitive elements come to the fore with the more recent forms, in which teams and individuals are pitted against each other or natural obstacles in an artificial environment created specifically for the show. These are typified by programs such as *Survivors*, *Top Shot*, and *The Apprentice*, plus all the variants pitting chefs, mechanics, designers, beauty queens, and hairdressers against each other, while a stern host or presenter lectures them about the rules and team play, and announces who is "sent home" for failing to meet the challenges of the format.

Critics have complained about the "dumbing down" of mass media entertainment, and can point to such shows as *Are You Smarter than a 5th Grader* and *Deal or No Deal* as prime examples of shows in which the level of intellectual effort is small or nonexistent, with pure chance as a major element in determining the "winners."

Finally, there are successful series on television that are essentially nothing but standard documentaries about exotic jobs and locations: *Ice Road Truckers*, *Ax Men*, *Dog, the Bounty Hunter*, *Pawn Stars*, *American Hoggers*, *Sons of Guns*, and the most successful of the genre, *Deadliest Catch*. These shows owe their success to three major components: an exotic location, charismatic individuals followed by the camera, and a structured narrative (complete with music cues) that makes routine activity into high drama. Over the years, audiences came to identify strongly with the captains of the Alaskan fishing fleet in *Deadliest Catch*, to the point where there was mass mourning for a skipper who suffered a fatal heart attack during the series. As an unintended consequence, many of the people featured in these shows have become "famous," with their own shows, being guest stars in other venues, and acquiring all the trappings of soap opera stardom, without having to memorize lines. Cultural historian Daniel Boorstin defines this sort of popular fame or stardom as "being well known for being well-known."

A compelling subgenre of this is the exploitation of the criminal justice system, exemplified by *48 Hours* and *Lockup*, in which the viewing public is either voyeur or participant in the apprehension and incarceration of real criminals (who have all signed releases).

It's safe to say that anything that fascinates viewers can be grist for the reality show: a partial list includes paranormal activity and "psychics"; Penn & Teller's *Bullshit*, which exposes the techniques behind "the sell" or "the pitch" of these shows; and more benevolent explorations of science and popular beliefs, such as *Mythbusters*.

Because of the number of shows being produced and the amount of time it takes to shoot, edit, and present them, there are a huge number of employment opportunities, in both the entry and executive levels. Every talent and ability is required, from production staff to shoot and record the programs, to the planning and postproduction that add structure and episodic quality, to the countless hours of raw material captured by the cameras.

All the lessons of documentary production apply here, as well as a special set of cautions that is peculiar to the genre. Working in reality programming is a great way to learn, but it's exhausting and usually underpaid and exploitative in every category. The owners and producers who originate or license the format do very well, and great fortunes have been built for some. Many programs began small, in other countries, and were successfully imported to the US as network entertainment, then repurposed and sold back to the originating venues at much higher license fees.

For the people who actually shoot and edit and work on the shows, it's important to understand that it's not a ticket into the big time; on the contrary, for most people it's a path to burnout and exhaustion. The production jobs are rarely unionized (the editors are an exception), and the drivers, assistants, interns, and other worker bees are expected to routinely work eighty-hour weeks without overtime. As of this edition, the WGA and DGA are making strong efforts to organize the form but so far have met with little success. If you find yourself employed on a reality show, please reread the chapters on taking care of yourself and working in documentaries.

In conclusion, anything that can be filmed or recorded can be made into entertainment. Anything that's entertaining can be sold. Anything that can be sold can generate an income for the creators and rights-holders. It's in your interest as a boss, writer, director, actor, or craftsperson to remember a nameless South

Sea Islander who told an inquiring anthropologist, "We don't have any art; we just do everything as well as we can."

If the result of your work is art, it's to your credit. If it's entertainment, that's also of inestimable value. For the artist or creator, the process can be its own reward. Just do it all as well as you can, and you'll never be disappointed. You will make mistakes, of course, but you might also make a living, or a fortune. We hope you've found our words useful, and we certainly wish you the best. Thanks for your time.

The Character Profile Worksheet for Actors

Who am I _____

(Your name/your character's name)

Age _____

(Your age/your character's age)

What do I want? (Objective/Intention) _____

_____

(Your/your character's immediate need from the other person—
or for himself or herself)

Action or Activity _____

(What do I do to get what I want?)

Obstacle _____

(Something that stops you from getting what you want)

Secrets _____

(What does your character privately know that the others don't?)

Before- and After Moment _____

(What just happened before your entrance, where are you going when you exit?)

Arc _____

(How does the character change or evolve from the beginning of the scene to the end?)

Beats _____

(List the moments when one character's objective either succeeds or fails, and then transitions to become the next beat.)

Overall story arc _____

(Describe the beginning, middle, and end of the entire piece, both with your character's involvement and generally, in story terms.)

Intentions/Objectives
for the Actor
(in alphabetical order)

to be **adamant**

to **amuse**

to **analyze**

to **annoy**

to **argue**

to **avoid**

to **become free**

to **boast**

to **brush off**

to **calm**

to **challenge**

to **chastise**

to **cheer up**

to **comfort**

to **complain**

to be **compulsive**

to **confide**

to be **confident**

to **cover your feelings**

to **daydream**

to **daze**

to **destroy**

to **discredit**

to **disrespect someone**

to **dream of**

to **drive 'em mad**

to **educate**

to **entertain**

to **exaggerate**

to **explain**

to **feel sorry**
to **feel sorry for yourself**
to **flirt**
to be **friendly**
to **gain composure**
to **gain control**
to **get attention**
to **get rid of someone or something**
to **get sympathy**
to **get your point across**
to **goof off**
to **gossip**
to **idolize**
to **ignore**
to **impress**
to be **inflexible**
to **inform**
to be **innocent**
to **internalize**
to be **intimate**
to **intimidate**
to be **jealous**
to **joke**
to **justify**
to **let in on a secret (whisper/draw in)**

to **make someone feel guilty**
to **make someone love you**
to **mesmerize**
to **mock**
to **not understand**
to be **oblivious**
to **plead**
to **pout**
to **praise**
to **put yourself down**
to **put off**
to **question**
to **remember**
to **seduce**
to be **self-righteous**
to **show superiority**
to **sneak away**
to be **stubborn**
to **tease (make fun of)**
to **tell a story**
to **tell off**
to **threaten**
to **tickle**
to **understand**
to **warn**
to **work it out**
to be **worried**

A Simple Glossary of Actors Terminology, for Directors and Other Bosses

arc. The beginning/middle/end of a scene within a larger context, or (in screenwriting) the shape of the story (also "beginning/middle/end," but in a larger sense—e.g., "The voyage, trials, and triumphant return of an adventurer to his home and family; see *The Odyssey*).

backstory. The unseen history of a character or situation prior to the moments expressed in the text, sometimes expressed in exposition.

beat. A breath, a pause, an entire moment or paragraph, or a section of the narrative. Beats have different meanings for directors, writers, and actors, although sometimes they coincide.

before-and after-life moments. The actor's understanding of where his or her character was immediately before his or her entrance, and where he or she is bound after exit.

core. The central and defining element of a character that informs and directs his or her behavior. See also *spine*.

exposition. The conveying of the history (or backstory) in dialogue ("I could've been a contender," says Terry Malloy in *On the Waterfront*) or in images ("The camera lingers on a trophy and a photo on the wall showing the character in her youth").

intention. What do you want the other character in the scene to do for you, or you for them? Used as a synonym for *objective*.

layering and covering. Additional behaviors and character traits that may be explicitly shown, but that conceal or add texture to a character's core by being different from what's specifically stated. (Example: the merciless killer who paints toy soldiers for children as a hobby.)

obstacles. Story elements that interfere with the completion of characters' intentions.

secret. Something that only the character knows; something not conveyed in backstory or exposition.

spine. The core structure of the character; the "backbone"; the sum of the many parts and hints in the text that add up to the central and constant theme that defines who the character truly is. See also *core*.

surprise. An actor's trick, in which an action or gesture is saved before performance and "sprung" on the other actor(s) in the action, with the intention of creating a spontaneous response that adds to the reality and believability of the scene.

underbelly. The text that's not spoken; a parallel meaning or elaboration on the script in the character or actor's own words; an understanding that underlies or supports the specificity of the text. Used as a synonym for **subtext**.

the "Ws": Who, Why, What. These are similar to the requirements of the lead paragraph in a news story, in which the entire story is summed up in *who, what, why, where, when*, and *how*. In acting, this is the breakdown: *who* are you talking to, *why* are you talking to them, *what* do you want from them, *what* will you do to get it, and *what* will you do if you get it (or don't)? (The *how, when*, and *where* is exposition and implicit in the cinematography and story.)

Back Life History Worksheet

Start with appendix A for the basics, and then expand upon your character's life experiences. "Character is destiny," and who you are is the sum total of all that's happened to you. These are some examples; add to them, explore them, keep a journal with these notes and your "colors" (things or memories from your life that move you).

History

1. Where and how did you spend your childhood?
2. How and where were you educated?
3. Membership: clubs, organizations, gangs, musical groups?
4. Did you have pets?
5. What were your favorite activities?
6. What incident or event (if any) changed your youth?

Present Time

1. Do you have a job or regular employment?

2. How do you feel about it?

3. Are you in love? Married? In a relationship? "Other"?

4. Do you exercise, work out, keep fit?

5. Are you involved in self-improvement via therapy, yoga, or some other system?

Sensory Triggers

1. What smells, sights, sounds, touches and textures, and tastes interest you?

2. Which of the above are addictive or superpleasant to you?

3. Which of the above disgust or repel you?

4. Why?

A Viewer's Filmography:
A No-Win Situation

Lists are subjective; there are film directories with tens of thousands of titles, many of them assigned a genre or style. It's useful to have bound copies in your library of reference books such as *Leonard Maltin's Classic Movie Guide* or Mick Martin and Marcia Porter's *DVD and Video Guide*, and *The Golden Retriever* guides edited by Martin Conners and Jim Craddock. Then, of course, there's good old IMDB.com: the most exhaustive list of world films and credits on the Internet. The American Film Institute has come up with the AFI "Top 100" in a number of categories: horror, comedy, and so forth. Other reputable organizations have their own lists, and the US Library of Congress has designated hundreds of films as worthy of preservation for all time. Every fan site and movie enthusiasts' web pages and blogs carry untold numbers of titles for "must see" viewing; everyone's an authority. We aren't immune—we've accumulated a list of hundreds of significant titles that we think everyone should see, and if you're honest, you'll confess to having your own list of films and television shows that everyone should see or at least know, and you'll have opinions as to why. You may notice there are very few films from the twenty-first century here. Not because we haven't recently been to the movies, but because the films made since 2000 are part of your present experience, and (we hope) you've seen the small, independent works, as well as the top-grossing box office successes. This is a cultural literacy exercise, not a "greatest hits" compilation.

Every published list is incomplete the moment it's published. In the English-speaking world, at least five hundred new films are released annually, and another few thousand independent features are produced but never see distribution. What we've done here is make arbitrary selections based on our own knowledge and preferences. Feel free to add or subtract your own favorites and assign them where you will. If we've made what you believe to be any egregious errors or omissions, write to us so that we may amend the list in future editions.

This is a raw list; we haven't subdivided it into genre or subtypes. As an exercise though, you might want to assign every film listed (that you've seen) to one or more of the many possible categories. Some films might fit in a number of categories (e.g., *Casino* is a gangster film, a character-driven drama, and an example of subjective narrative).

Keep in mind the realities of the marketplace for new productions. Most films on lists are so dated that they are historical curiosities, significant only to film scholars and enthusiasts. Young and entry-level filmmakers may never get the opportunity to make a big-budget studio version of a Broadway musical or a feature-length animation with movie-star voices, or be employed to make a tent-pole action spectacle with a budget in excess of $100 million. The same goes for genres that may have permanently passed from style with modern filmgoers: classic Westerns, biblical epics, pirate movies, and all-star ensemble dramas. Luckily, some of these have found their way onto cable television with more controlled budgets, where they perpetuate traditional cinematic styles and offer a chance for new directors to work in classic forms.

You may have noticed there's nothing much in the book about animation, a genre that's still thriving after almost a hundred years, with some of the most creative work being done in modern theatrical features. With the exception of very short films and student projects, the resources necessary for the new theatrical-feature animation typified by Pixar and Disney remains generally out of reach of the beginning filmmaker (a careless statement; some new technology may render this last assertion meaningless. We hope so—you readers deserve a break, and a forum for your fresh ideas!)

Some Genres and Categories (Make Your Own Lists or Categories)

animation

contemporary drama (set in the "present")

coming of age

documentary (including "mockumentaries")

fantasy
film noir
historical drama (set in a
    period or the past)
horror
internal narrative
light erotica
love story/romance
musical
outrageous comedy

police procedural
religious
romantic comedy
science fiction
screwball comedy
slapstick comedy
social and political
    commentary
spectacle
westerns

The Authors' Arbitrary List
for Film Literacy

1. *12 Angry Men*
2. *2001: A Space Odyssey*
3. *3 Days of the Condor*
4. *The 39 Steps*
5. *The 400 Blows*
6. *42nd Street*
7. *47 Ronin (Chusingura)*
8. *48 Hours*
9. *8 ½*
10. *A Boy and His Dog*
11. *A Bronx Tale*
12. *The Adventures of Pluto Nash*
13. *The Adventures of Robin Hood*
14. *A Few Good Men*
15. *A Man and a Camera* (Russian)
16. *A Man and a Woman*
17. *A Man for All Seasons*
18. *The Apartment*
19. *A Passage to India*
20. *A Star Is Born (Garland version)*

368. *Titanic*
369. *To Have and To Have Not*
370. *To Kill a Mockingbird*
371. *Tootsie*
372. *Training Day*
373. *Trapeze*
374. *The Treasure of Sierra Madre*
375. *Triumph of the Will* (German)
376. *The Truman Show*
377. *The Turning Point*
378. *Twilight Zone: The Movie*
379. *Two for the Road*
380. *The Verdict*
381. *Vertigo*
382. *Viva Zapata*
383. *Waiting for Guffman*
384. *Walkabout*
385. *The Wall*
386. *War and Peace*
387. *The War of the Worlds*
388. *The Way We Were*
389. *The Wedding Singer*
390. *West Side Story*
391. *Whatever Happened to Baby Jane*
392. *The Wild Bunch*
393. *The Wild One*
394. *Wings of Desire*
395. *The Witches of Eastwick*
396. *The Wizard of Oz*
397. *The Wolfman* (1966)
398. *Wuthering Heights*
399. *Yi Yi*
400. *Young Frankenstein*
401. *Z*
402. *Zelig*
403. *Zorba the Greek*